Creating Healing Relationships is enjoyable to read and I found it difficult to put down—something new and interesting appeared on every page. It also cleared up numerous gray areas for me and will serve as a useful reference for my practice. I'm so pleased to see the emphasis on the importance of maintaining self-care and personal awareness for healing practitioners!

—Linnie Thomas, HTCP, HTCI, MLM, author of *The Encyclopedia of Energy Medicine* and founder of the International Association for Energy Healers

Creating Healing Relationships is an excellent resource for understanding the ethics and professional standards involved in the practice of energy healing and will be a helpful guide to all who seek to develop successful energy therapy practices. Dorothea skillfully defines terms that are often confused, such as morals, principles, values, and ethics, and demonstrates how professional standards emerge from these concepts. Her compassionate style, wealth of experience, and fascinating discussions make the book easy to read and integrate.

—Maria Becker, MD, FRCP(C) Youth Psychiatry, Member Emeritus of the College of Physicians and Surgeons of Ontario; Director of Ethics and Professional Affairs, the Association for Comprehensive Energy Psychology (ACEP); author of children's books

Personal and relationship integrity are the foundation for serving clients and communities in healing ways. Energy therapies have an uncanny ability to unlock our human capacity for hyper-growth with potency and speed, which makes impeccable practitioner ethics essential. This book illuminates the key ethical principles and professional standards to guide energy therapy practitioners. For the sake of your own heart's wellbeing, your work with your clients, and deepening the credibility of energy therapies as their visibility mushrooms, let this book be a beacon for navigating the expanded ethical dimensions that are involved when using energy therapies.

—David Gruder, PhD, DCEP, Psychologist, award-winning author, Executive Director of Integrity Revolution, and Co-Founder/Founding President of ACEP

This book serves as an educator and inclusive guide for those who are involved in caring professions. Dorothea skillfully aligns with integrity and truth in the most practical and resourceful manner. This book is the ethical roadmap for all energy practitioners.

I am honored to have my name associated with this wonderful text!

—Harriet Mall, PhD, psychologist, counselor, healer/Chair, Ethics Committee, ACEP

Creating Healing Relationships

Professional Standards for Energy Therapy Practitioners

Dorothea Hover-Kramer, EdD, RN, CNS, DCEP

Foreword by Cyndi Dale

www.DorotheaLifeArtist.com.

Energy Psychology Press
Santa Rosa, CA 95404
www.energypsychologypress.com

Hover-Kramer, Dorothea.
  Creating healing relationships : professionsl standards for energy therapy practitioners
/ by Dorothea Hover-Kramer — 1st ed.
    p. cm.
  Includes bibliographical references and index.
  ISBN: 978-1-60415-080-3 (hard cover)
  1. Mind and body therapies. 2. Therapist and patient. I. Title.
  [DNLM: 1. Mind-Body Therapies—standards. 2. Mind-Body Therapies—ethics.
3. Professional Practice—standards. 4. Professional-Patient Relations. WB 880]
  RC489.M53H679 2011
  616.89'1—dc22

                                    2011012413
                        Copyright © 2011, Dorothea Hover-Kramer

Cover design by Victoria Valentine
Typesetting by Karin Kinsey
Editing by Stephanie Marohn
Typeset in Adobe Garamond Pro and Eva
Printed in USA
First Edition

10 9 8 7 6 5 4 3 2 1

*Anyone who is not working toward the truth
is missing the whole point of living.*
—Buddha

This book is dedicated to those who seek the human truth of caring
for others in their lives and who, by doing so, also bring healing
to themselves and the wider world.

Contents

About the Author..xi

About This Book xiii

Acknowledgments xvi

Foreword, by Cyndi Dale xvii

SECTION I: BASIC PRACTICE
CONSIDERATIONS FOR ENERGY THERAPY PRACTITIONERS

Chapter 1: From Personal Values to Professional
Standards and Public Recognition 25

Chapter 2: The Context for Energy Therapies in
Healthcare Today... 35

Chapter 3: Legal Considerations and Risk Management 47

Vignettes for Section I.. 55

SECTION II: WALKING YOUR TALK—
STANDARDS FOR ESTABLISHING AND MAINTAINING A HEALTHY
RELATIONSHIP WITH YOURSELF AS A PRACTITIONER

Chapter 4: Why Care of Self Is Primary 63

Chapter 5: Learning from Personal Interferences 75

Chapter 6: Increasing Practitioner Insights with the Chakras 87

Chapter 7: Extending Practitioner Energies to Include
Intuitive and Transpersonal Domains 103

Vignettes for Section II.. 111

SECTION III: STANDARDS FOR
CREATING HEALING RELATIONSHIPS WITH CLIENTS

Chapter 8: The Fiduciary Relationship in Energy Therapies 123

Chapter 9: Client Considerations in
Energy Therapy Interventions...................................... 137

Chapter 10: Addressing Clients'
Nonordinary States of Consciousness 149

Chapter 11: The Sacred Contract Between
                 Caregiver and Client 163

Vignettes for Section III 175

SECTION IV: STANDARDS FOR CREATING
HEALING RELATIONSHIPS WITH COLLEAGUES, OTHER HEALTHCARE
PROFESSIONALS, AND IN OUR COMMUNITIES

Chapter 12: Building Bridges for Innovative Approaches 187
Chapter 13: Developing the Professional Image
                 of Energy Modalities.. 199

Vignettes for Section IV.. 209

CONCLUSION

Chapter 14: Future Developments as Energy Therapies Mature......217

Appendix A: Further Recommended Reading 227
Appendix B: Sample Forms 229
Appendix C: Leading Energy Therapy Professional Associations......233

Endnotes.. 237
Glossary 243
Index.. 249

Case History Vignettes

Section I

Vignette I.1 Assuming Clients Are Willing
Vignette I.2 Client Chooses Not to Receive More Energy Interventions

Section II

Vignette II.1 Behind Schedule All Too Often!
Vignette II.2 Missing the Most Important Part
Vignette II.3 Holding Center in the Face of Adversity
Vignette II.4 All Boxed In!
Vignette II.5 Overcoming Practitioner Resistance
Vignette II.6 "Where is God When I need Him/Her?"
Vignette II.7 What Did I Get Myself Into?

Section III

Vignette III.1 The Drama Triangle Redux
Vignette III.2 Here Comes the Judge
Vignette III.3 History Becomes Too Alive
Vignette III.4 Avoiding Avoidance
Vignette III.5 Departure Without Comment
Vignette III.6 Client Needs Exactly What Is Rejected
Vignette III.7 Passivity, Inc.

Section IV

Vignette IV.1 Hearing Bad News about Another Practitioner
Vignette IV.2 Finding a Good Practitioner
Vignette IV.3 Helping an Indecisive Client
Vignette IV.4 Dual Relationship: Renter and Provider of Care
Vignette IV.5 Potential Dual Relationship—Writer's Group
Vignette IV.6 Handling a Client's Secret

Exercises, Tables, and Illustrations

Illustration 4.1 Human Biofield and Related Chakras

Illustration 4.2 Sample Image of Interactive Biofield —
Practitioner and Client

Exercise 4.1 Sample Centering Practice

Exercise 4.2 Sample Self-Assessment of Your Personal Energies

Exercise 5.1 Ongoing Checklist for Self-reflection

Exercise 5.2 Solar Imagery to Nurture the Chakras and Biofield

Table 6.1 Overview of the Chakras and Their Psychological Functions

Table 6.2 Resources for Addressing Chakra Vulnerabilities

Exercise 7.1 Accessing Internal Dialogue

Exercise 8.1 Tracking Right Use of Power in Relation to Clients

Table 10.1 Continuum of Major Levels of Consciousness

Exercise 14.1 Checklist for Establishing Healthy Relationships in Your
Energy Practice

About the Author

Dorothea Hover-Kramer, EdD, RN, DCEP (diplomate in comprehensive energy psychology), has been a clinical nurse specialist and clinical psychologist in private practice for more than thirty years. Much of her practice fosters mind-body-spirit integration, and energetic interventions to create a unique blend of creative possibilities for her clients are a vital part of her practice. She is director of Behavioral Health Consultants in Port Angeles, Washington, and gives presentations and workshops nationally and internationally.

Dr. Hover-Kramer served on the leadership council of the American Holistic Nurses Association for ten years and then helped to pioneer work in Healing Touch more than twenty years ago. She is a recognized founding elder of the Healing Touch Program. She cofounded the Association for Comprehensive Energy Psychology (ACEP) in 1999 to empower psychotherapists and professionals from many disciplines to use energetic modalities. She also served as president of the Association and became one of the leading architects of ACEP's certification program, which reaches counselors and allied healthcare professionals worldwide.

Dorothea is the author of eight other books about energy therapies, which include six textbooks for energy practitioners and two books for the public, *Second Chance at Your Dream: Engaging Your Body's Energy Resources for Optimal Aging, Creativity, and Health* (2009) and *Healing Touch: Essential Energy Medicine for Yourself and Others* (2011).

On the personal side, Dorothea lives with her husband and numerous pets on the North Olympic Peninsula where she often sails, gardens, performs with chamber music groups, and produces visual arts. She is the mother of three talented adult children and grandmother of seven lively grandchildren. She is also a community activist and serves on several environmental and medical non-profit boards.

About This Book

Creating Healing Relationships: Professional Standards for Energy Therapy Practitioners is a new version that greatly updates and expands on an earlier work Dorothea wrote with contributions from attorney Midge Murphy in 2005 under the title of *Creating Right Relationships: A Practical Guide to Ethics in Energy Therapies.* The book underwent several updates and was published by Behavioral Health Consultants, with repeated printings over the past five years.

In late 2010, Dawson Church, PhD, energy medicine researcher, author of the best-selling *The Genie in Your Genes,* and publisher of Energy Psychology Press, asked Dorothea to write this new book on professional ethical standards for energy therapy practitioners who come from many differing backgrounds and skill levels. Because of her increased attention to practice issues and dilemmas, Dorothea was able to complete the book quite rapidly. Both she and the publisher hope the book will bring practical insights and resources to the growing ranks of energy therapy practitioners.

The book is divided into four major sections. The first includes basic information for practitioners on considerations in practice, from personal values to ethical and professional standards and public recognition, the place and challenges of energy therapies within Complementary and Alternative Medicine (CAM) in the United States, and a brief look at essential legal considerations and risk management practices.

The second section addresses practitioner self-care and ways to foster a healthy relationship with oneself in preparation for interaction with clients.

The third section discusses client care considerations, including essentials for successful practice and special needs such as handling intuited material, archetypes that emerge in the intimacy of an energetic relationship, and the reality of clients' nonordinary states of consciousness.

The last section explores the creation of healthy relatedness with colleagues, other professionals, and communities. The concluding chapter opens doors to looking at future developments possible within energy therapies and their increasing presence on the healthcare scene.

Establishing communicative language to discuss the broad topic without precedents in professional standards is always a challenge. It is important to write from a comprehensive perspective that encompasses the needs of energy healing practitioners with diverse backgrounds and skills. My intention is to reach both licensed and unlicensed people who are developing an individual or integrated group practice in an energy modality. This population includes a large number of allied health caregivers, psychotherapists, counselors, social workers, nurses, physicians, addictions specialists, intuitive healers, body workers, massage therapists, and laypersons.

The fact that you are reading this book is a sign of the growing professionalism you seek within your practice, and I will address you, the reader, with the respect and caring due a fellow professional. If you are not yet used to thinking of yourself as a professional in the healing art you've chosen, please do so now as you consider the ideas shared here.

The ideal word for the one who extends human caring to another is "practitioner." The word "client" describes the recipient of services in nonmedical settings and "patient" is the term for receivers in medical settings. To make the text flow, I've used other synonyms for practitioner such as "caregiver," "helper," "facilitator," "therapist," and "advocate," although these titles may not quite fit the wording that best describes your practice.

As always, the English language poses potentials for awkwardness by demanding gender-specific pronouns. Since both practitioners and clients can be of either gender, I alternate masculine and feminine pronouns to lend impartiality and clarity. I use the first-person plural pronouns (we, us, our) to refer to all of us who are practitioners involved in the joys, challenges, and learning associated with one or more forms of energy healing work.

At the end of each section are vignettes to illustrate the topics covered in that section. The vignettes depict actual situations that have arisen in practice. Names and specifics have, of course, been changed to guard confidentiality.

Acknowledgments

The insights and understandings of many people have come together to support this book. First of all, I want to thank Dawson Church, PhD, of Energy Psychology Press, who invited this book with his unrelenting energies.

I'd also like to thank my helpful volunteer reviewers for accuracy and depth:

- Maria Becker, MD, Director of Ethics and Professional Affairs, ACEP

- Cynthia Hutchison, DNSc, RN, HTCP/I, Program Director of the Healing Touch Program

- Linnie Thomas, HTCP/I and author of *The Encyclopedia of Energy Medicine* and IAFEH founder

I also want to express appreciation to Courtney Arnold and the entire staff of Energy Psychology Press, who were always directly helpful in the book production process.

Finally, I want to acknowledge and honor the readers of this book because they will be the pioneers in shaping what energy therapies become in the healthcare field. As they understand and come to value their strengths and the need for professional standards of practice, our field will grow and mature.

—Dorothea Hover-Kramer, Port Angeles, WA, March 2011

Foreword

I was raised in a family of doctors and, since childhood, knew I wanted to be a healer. As far as my family was concerned, the path was well defined. I would attend medical school, skip a few years of sleep, and emerge with a white coat. For all that, I'd proudly wear a lapel with the initials "MD" after my name.

The advantages of this course were fairly obvious. My reputation secure, I'd start a practice that would flourish. How could I not create a business that would help people? Thousands had grooved this riverbed; I had only to follow procedure and do my best to succeed. Already provided were crystal-clear guidelines for interacting with clients, as well as legal and institutional protocols clarifying diagnostic, treatment, and financial activities. If I couldn't help someone, my training would assist me with recommending other resources.

Almost every licensed discipline functions the same way. Therapists, nurses, doctors, technicians—these care providers receive the proper training and are then able to hang out their shingle, either working for or running respected practices. Clients are guaranteed a clear set of expectations, and the professional, knowledge of the rules. This system affords safety and assurance for healer and client alike, the rules operating like buffers on the sides of a bowling lane. They keep everyone and everything rolling the right way. The problem—the opportunity—is that there are other, nonallopathic versions of medicine, many of which are just as (and sometimes more) effective than conventional Western practices. These methods include energy medicine, also known as energy healing and energy therapy.

I happened to enter the healing field through the byway of energy healing rather than the highway of conventional medicine. My training included bushwhacking through jungles to engage shamans, medicine people, and natural healers; reading books about quantum physics, psychology, and ancient spiritualities; and attending classes on intuition, religion, and alternative healing. I was fortunate. My experiences resulted in a thriving practice and the publication of over a dozen books.

Yet, throughout these twenty-five years of flowing along the veins instead of arteries of health care, I have struggled with the very issues addressed in this amazing, insightful, and necessary book by Dorothea Hover-Kramer, *Creating Healing Relationships: Professional Standards for Energy Therapy Practitioners.* I have sought *all these* years for a guide like this very one, a book outlining the ethical and operational necessities of serving as an energy specialist. And here it is, the practical advice needed to bolster the energy worker's confidence, performance, and safety. The list of questions we energy healers must ask ourselves about our values, ethics, needs, standards, and professional codes of conduct are overwhelming, and yet they are intelligently and compassionately surfaced by Dorothea. Set aside the reality that the profession is thousands of years old. Ignore the fact that scientific evidence is documenting its raison d'etre (and frequently audacious effectiveness.) Overlook the fact that energy therapy is one of the fastest growing arms of medicine, both as a stand-alone field and a component of complementary and integrative health care. Energy therapy is, quite simply, a new profession in the Western world. Consequently, our discipline lacks the structure and protocol afforded licensed medical disciplines.

Being young isn't easy, especially for the practitioner involved in the emerging field. There are a lot of questions and fewer answers. The first challenge is explaining the trade to others. Even Gabe, my twelve-year-old, who has grown up with an energy-working mom, recently asked me:

"Exactly what do you do, Mom?"

I sat back, puzzled as to how to explain my job in a way that wouldn't create havoc in the reductionist world of sixth-grade boys.

"Well, what do you think?" I hedged.

"Well, I think you're kind of like a therapist, maybe a doctor, except you talk to God more and most of what you do is invisible." He paused. "Can I have lunch now?"

How do you tell people that, as an energy practitioner, you "open infinity?" That's right. We're the people who direct the infinite, loving healing energy of the universe to help our clients.

This simple identity of an energy healer causes enormous problems for practitioner and client alike. Dorothea brings this situation to the forefront and addresses it. What outcomes can the practitioner guarantee when working with energies that are often unseen, inaudible, and immeasurable? What are reasonable expectations for a client in terms of benefits?

Conventional care providers can't ensure results either, although they are pretty good at offering statistical averages. They can, however, outline their protocol, which provides a safety net for practitioners and clients. Dorothea suggests that there are ways that energy therapy practitioners can do the same, creating maps that we and our clients can follow on the quest for well-being.

Another challenge facing energy healers is the sheer number of energetic methodologies. The purist focuses energy via intention through the energetic anatomy, a complex set of energy channels, centers, and fields. Having said this, there are hundreds of practices that are energetic in nature but labeled and packaged with different terms. The short list includes homeopathy, Healing Touch, faith healing, hands-on healing, intuitive consulting, diet and nutritional healing, vibrational medicine, aromatherapy, Reiki, prayer, acupuncture, yoga, medical qigong, body-mind methods, meditation, chiropractic, massage, herbalism, naturopathy, Ayurvedic medicine, and many spiritual, shamanic practices. How can we develop codes of conduct for a discipline that is so wide-ranging?

Ready to add another layer of difficulty? The fact is that there are a lot of licensed conventional practitioners now employing energy medicine in their practices. They might look like Clark Kent, but, every so often, out comes the Super Energy Cape. How does a "regular" health-care professional best interweave an energetic modality into his or her practice? What's the best way to incorporate energetic treatments and how the heck do you explain what you're doing to the client? Or *should* you? Is it ethical to "send energy" or even pray for someone and not tell them?

I've only scratched the initial challenges that the contemporary energy practitioner confronts, all of which are faced down by Dorothea, who doesn't turn from the charging bull but, rather, waves the Super Energy Cape (it's red) in front of us until we ask for answers. As she attests, we *must* adopt a set of standards equivalent to or even higher than those followed by our conventional friends. To do less would be to ignore the power of the infinite, to shy away from our calling as healers. To become more accepted and understood is to be invited to help more people. We're also allowed to continually develop our gifts, which is one of the most exciting activities in the world.

Dorothea's book assesses nearly every predicament (and opportunity, for aren't these often the same?) facing the energy therapist in terms of our heartfelt values that guide us to professional standards and codes of conduct. The plethora of issues addressed is vast and deep. Dorothea covers legal considerations, including risk management, the proper use of touch, financial responsibilities, marketing messages, and protocol for avoiding malpractice, negligence, and fraud. She probes client-care questions, including the provision for client confidentiality, treatment plans, referrals, and the management of client expectations. She also discusses an often-overlooked aspect of energy therapies and all medical method-ologies: the management of our self-care.

For me, this last area has presented more challenges than any other. I'm a giver, which means that I've been a raving codependent from birth onward. I've had compassion fatigue more often than a toddler catches the common cold. While I've always worked on my own issues, I'm also terribly good at working on others' issues, often giving clients my own energies rather than drawing on the unlimited supply of universal energy. Aptly, Dorothea instructs us in how to care for ourselves so we can care for others.

In the end, one of the most sage pieces of wisdom she offers is this: while we all strive personally to develop and uphold our morals and professionalism, we do this through establishing caring, healthy relationships. We are ultimately called to respect our own unique path, as well as the paths of others.

To care for the self includes recognizing that whatever our background or training, licensure or lack thereof, we are healers, just as doctors, counselors, and dentists are. We are medics, caretakers, heart menders, and soul soothers. We are searchers of truth and upholders of goodness. We are people of love called to encourage wellness, deliver hope, and prevent tragedy. We are people who seek to relate to the universe—the Divine, higher power, One, Creator, Goodness—in order to offer our gifts to those who need them. We accomplish this through caring, the nourishing of spirit within ourselves and others.

—Cyndi Dale, Bloomington, MN, January 2011

Cyndi Dale is the author of the best-selling books The Subtle Body: An Encyclopedia of Your Energetic Anatomy *and* The Complete Book of Chakra Healing, *published in fourteen countries. She has provided intuitive consulting and energy healing for over 30,000 clients and loves to help people perceive their true brilliance and access their inner healing powers.*

SECTION I:

BASIC PRACTICE CONSIDERATIONS FOR ENERGY THERAPY PRACTITIONERS

CHAPTER ONE

FROM PERSONAL VALUES TO PROFESSIONAL STANDARDS AND PUBLIC RECOGNITION

The heart is where the beauty of the human spirit comes alive...When you feel for someone, you become united with that person in an intimate way; your concern and compassion come alive, drawing some of the other person's world and spirit into yours...Without the ability to feel, friendship and love could never be born....
—John O'Donohue, poet and philosopher[1]

Caring for one another being is certainly a most endearing human trait. Reaching out to help others, even people we don't already know, is one of life's most rewarding endeavors. The wealth of knowledge that is accumulated from the social sciences and healing arts teaches the value of altruism and generosity because they reward both the one who gives caring and the one who receives it. They also help to bring harmony to human society. Yet, most current settings of medical and social services are abundant with forms, abstractions, and computerized and high-tech interventions, with a notable absence of heart-centered caring.

As an effort to counteract this trend, energy therapies have emerged to champion healthy, healing interrelationships that have come to be increasingly valued by a resourceful and creative public. Instead of piecemeal medical care and "parts-oriented" bureaucratic systems, large numbers of consumers now seek holistic, integrative care that addresses the whole person. Energy therapy practitioners are beginning to fill a much-needed void in today's healthcare.

To validate and give credibility to this newly emerging field, it is essential to define its humanistic values, the related ethic of client-centered care, and the implied professional standards that emerge from core values in human caring. Within most of the more than two hundred emerging energy modalities, however, personal and professional standards are assumed—not codified, written, or fully described. This book is therefore an exploration to help define the customary and necessary standards that are needed as guidelines for practitioners who engage in this new pioneering field of endeavor.

Beyond being in compliance with legal and regulatory considerations, practitioners of energy therapies make a deep commitment to creating, establishing, and maintaining healing relationships with clients who entrust themselves to their care. Additionally, to support high levels of care, they also create healthy, positive connections to themselves and to the communities in which they live and work.

What Is Energy Therapy?

"Energy therapy," "energy healing," and the newer term "energy medicine" are all descriptive names for the many specific approaches to human caring that bring about relief of client symptoms by utilizing one or more aspects of the human energy system. There are wide variations in the actual methods applied by practitioners, but all of them aim to bring balance and harmony to perceived disturbances in clients' subtle energy systems.

Work with subtle energies can include focus on the meridian pathways that have been known in China for over five thousand years. Acupuncture, acupressure, and other forms of stimulating meridian acupoints have been found effective in bringing about physical and emotional relief. Other effective practices for establishing mind-body balance are based on Eastern traditions of working with the energy field or sheath (also called the biofield) that surrounds the human body and its related energy centers, called *chakras*. Existence of the biofield, the meridians, and the chakras is now well-documented by scientific investigations.

They can be sensed and measured within and around the human body in their nonmaterial, vibrational, and electromagnetic forms.[2]

Numerous energy therapy modalities also work with less well-known aspects of the subtle human energies, such as various flows, the electromagnetic grid, or repatterning fields, which are noted by sensitive, skilled practitioners. Most modalities teach some form of centering or alignment with the energetic resources of nature or the unifying consciousness of the universal energy field or force field.

For her groundbreaking work, *The Encyclopedia of Energy Medicine*,[3] Linnie Thomas interviewed proponents of the more than 250 energy medicine modalities currently practiced in the United States. This large aggregation of modalities reflects public interest in alternative resources for healthcare, especially for conditions that do not or cannot, for various reasons, respond to known offerings from conventional medical and psychological services.

Since the early seventies, nurses and allied healthcare professionals have implemented Therapeutic Touch in hospital and related medical settings to assist with pain relief and relaxation. Its assistance in physical problems such as chronic pain, degenerative conditions, and end-of-life challenges is visibly meeting the needs of the increasingly aging population. In 1989, Healing Touch joined the ranks and also became known as a viable complement to medical interventions. Both have been well documented and researched. Additionally, practitioners of both modalities are finding their methods effective in home-care settings, in treating minor injuries, in giving quick interventions in emergencies, in relieving trauma, and in coping with significant stages of the human life cycle.[4]

Following the public search for creative ways to resolve physical and emotional distress, numerous other energetic modalities have emerged in past decades and established training programs for their practitioners. Many of the modalities had their roots in long-standing philosophies of holistic care as conceived in Eastern orientations and such nations as China, India, Japan, and Russia. They come from a wide range of endogenous healing practices around the world. Sixty-five of the most known and established modalities are carefully presented in Thomas's encyclopedia under the broad categories labeled Eastern, Western, spiritual, and shamanic practices. An International Association for Energy Healers is forming under her leadership as well.[5]

Psychotherapists also brought energy concepts into their practices and pioneering work began in the 1980s with meridian-based interventions. The Association for Comprehensive Energy Psychology (ACEP)[6] was established in 1999 to bring together the large and growing family of therapies that encompass energetic treatment for emotional distress, anxiety, and trauma. Emotional Freedom Techniques (EFT)[7] is among the best-known practices in the new field that was named "energy psychology" by one of the discipline's leading authors, Dr. Fred Gallo.[8]

Many historical streams come together in the rapidly developing larger field now known as "energy medicine." Well-known and beloved practitioners and scientists have contributed the large variety of energetic approaches that serve to relieve both physical and psychological distress.[9, 10] In the next chapter, we'll explore the place of energy medicine within the national framework of complementary and alternative medicine (CAM).

Unique Aspects of Energy Modalities That Require Careful Practitioner Attention

Appropriate conduct toward oneself, clients, and other healthcare professionals calls for dedicated attention among energy practitioners. A major reason for this is the reality that we're operating within a new paradigm—one that is quite different from the linear thinking model that underlies most Western approaches. When we think of energy-based interventions, we recognize that nonlinear, nonreductionist, and nonmechanistic processes are involved. Since the human mind and body function more like a hologram—in multidimensional ways with many potentials at any given time—rather than like a mechanical object or computer, small changes in one area can become generalized throughout the physical, emotional, mental, and spiritual aspects of a client's system. A quick simile is to note how a minute change in temperature in one part of the ocean leads to outcomes in global climate such as the well-studied "El Niño effect."

The ethic of caring in the far-reaching parameters touched by energy therapies requires us to think beyond usual ideas of avoiding harm or focusing on what one should not do and to direct attention toward becoming genuinely client-centered. As practitioners, we have to recognize and understand the deep intimacy of energy field interactions with clients. Our verbal skills take a backseat to the reality of nonverbal communication that emanates from the practitioner's entire energy field and interacts with the client's. This mandates being mindful, respectful, cautious, and very clear about appropriate boundaries and knowing how best to use intuitional material, both from the client's and the practitioner's inner wisdom. Furthermore, we need to know how best to assist clients who connect to their transpersonal, spiritual dimensions and to deal with nonordinary states of consciousness that frequently surface during treatment sessions.

Thus the practice of energy therapies actually requires more rigorous attention from practitioners than would be required for someone engaging in cognitive talk psychotherapies or in administering conventional medical care. Since our field is so new, no national regulations or specific laws exist for governance of our professional endeavors. This reality does not mean that "anything goes"—rather it means that we as practitioners and pioneers are called and mandated to define and carefully build up the parameters of our profession. Unless this is done effectively to exceed what regulation from outside forces would achieve, we will not be able to maintain the present high levels of creativity and freedom we cherish. (The issues and challenges facing the profession, and all CAM modalities for that matter, are discussed more fully in the next chapter.)

Expanding from a Personal
Value System to Ethical Professional Standards of Care

The unique parameters of energy medicine draw practitioners to clarify their values, to know who they are in the world, and to define what they can realistically offer to clients. Based on personal and professional values, the guiding philosophy, principle, or ethic for client care becomes established. This valuing is not so much about deciding what is right or wrong behavior but, rather, about establishing agreed-upon guidelines for conducting oneself within the professional practice of an energy modality. Related and specific standards or models of practice spring from the recognized values and philosophy of each modality as it establishes itself and matures into professional standing.

To elaborate, we'll consider definitions of the operative terms as we explore the importance of professional standards. Many people tend to use interchangeably such terms as values, morals, laws, ethics, principles, standards, and professionalism. These terms are, in fact, quite different but operate in connection to each other and, in my experience, on a continuum that serves to inform practitioners.

- **Values** are intangible beliefs and highly regarded ideas that have become part of someone's essential personality. Integrity and honesty, for example, are abstract concepts that most children internalize as worthwhile qualities by age ten, especially when they recognize that others treat them better if they are honest and trustworthy. In energy therapies, core values are strong around respecting clients, trusting each individual's unique path, and engaging in positive self-care.

- **Morals** relate to judgment of human actions and character. Definitions of right and wrong evolve from strongly held morals to define "good" and "bad" behavior. Views of what is considered moral behavior may change over time as human society grows and changes. For example, slavery was considered acceptable in the eighteenth century as a necessary part of many cultures, while it is now officially eschewed and racist remarks are considered incorrect.

- **Principles** form the framework for personal and social integrity and arise from each person's core values. An energy practitioner's personal values to help those in need engender principles of compassion, acceptance, and healthy relatedness.

- **Ethics** is an expansion of principles to agreed and accepted behaviors for members of a group or organization. It is also the study of individual choices that influence relationships with others. Ethics deals with the moment-to-moment decisions one makes when no one is looking on. Ethics therefore exceeds behaviors that can be legally enforced. Many people, for example, drive differently when no police are visible, but a true ethic related to personal and passenger safety requires a watchful eye for reducing risks, driving within speed limits, stopping at amber lights, and so on. Ethics in energy therapies requires working with integrity, speaking truth kindly, and treating the therapeutic relationship with clients as a sacred contract.

- **Standards** are the practical manifestation of a profession's ethics and values. They constitute the specific expansion of ethical values and principles into defined behaviors and customary actions. For example, the ethic of truthfulness based on the principle of caring for others engenders the standard for making all representations and publicity about oneself honest and accurate, and to acknowledge accurately one's skills and limitations. Knowing one's limitations further leads to the standard of seeking consultation for complex client issues and having ample referral resources.

- **Professionalism** is the mark of a person whose attitudes, beliefs, and values are reflected in every interaction with others. In energy therapies, courtesy, consideration, conscientious endeavor to increase knowledge of one's field, and willingness to learn are hallmarks of a professional stance toward one's chosen career. Professional behaviors in energy work are supported by active commitment to bring client-centered values to life in each interaction with clients.

- **Laws** are codified rules of conduct agreed to by a municipality, county, state, region, or nation. Laws are enforced by officials and courts for the purpose of protecting the public's welfare. Laws exist because not all people behave in ethical ways, have positive values and clear principles, or operate under standards that build peace and harmony with others. Although practitioners of energy therapies are not likely to break laws knowingly, anyone who offers a service to the public is subject to the laws that govern businesses. Energy therapy practitioners thus need to know the laws that relate to their business practice and the implications for legal liabilities in their actions.

As we can see, there is a direct interrelationship between our essential values for helping others, our principles, which may include some moral judgments, and the ethic of caring. Caring is translated into standards for action that relate to and emerge from the values, principles, and ethics we espouse. As we consider identified standards of practice discussed in each section of this book, the entire field of energy medicine is empowered to increase orientation toward enhanced professionalism and public recognition.

* * * *

In this book, we'll look at the core value of creating healthy, healing, and caring relationships not only for our clients, but also for ourselves and our communities. The ethical principles are listed first in each section, followed by the most directly related professional standards. Then there are several chapters with supportive discussion and, finally, vignettes from real life to illustrate the ethical standards of care.

We'll complete our overview of basic considerations for energy therapy practitioners in the next two chapters before moving into the more specifically developed sections. In chapter 2, we look at the status of energy modalities within the large picture of today's healthcare. This will help us to appreciate the need for caution and carefully understood ethical professional standards for our innovative practices.

In chapter 3, we'll look at the major legal considerations and professional practice standards that need to flow from enacted legislation.

The value of client privacy, for example, has been codified with HIPPA legislation,[11] and practitioners therefore need to be aware of the client's right to confidentiality and privacy. They also need to know the arenas where most states mandate that confidentiality be subsumed to report or give warning of real or potential harm to appropriate agencies.

Chapter Two

The Context for Energy Therapies in Healthcare Today

A Brief History of Healing

5000 BC—I have an earache and go to see the village healer who gives me herbal teas and holds his hands over the ear. I feel better.

500 BC—I have an earache and go to the Greek dream temple where there is a drama about my problem with a chorus of advisors, known as theraps (the root for today's word "therapist"). All help me to feel better.

1870 AD—I have an earache and am advised to go to a surgeon who drains out the infection and I feel a lot of pain but later the ear is better.

1970 AD—I have an earache and am given an antibiotic and soon feel better.

2011 AD—I have an earache but the bacteria are resistant to all the antibiotics they can give me. I'm instructed to see an herbalist who gives me herbs and teas. I also visit a therapist who releases emotional issues related to the earache and consult with an energy medicine practitioner who passes her hands over my ears and body. I feel much better and also gain new insights about preventing future earaches.

—adapted from an anonymous quote circulated in holistic health meetings

The little parody given here summarizes some of the major phases in the evolution of medical care. It seems we've come full circle, back to traditional treatments such as herbs and hands-on interventions when usual medical approaches or medications do not work.

Although conventional Western medicine has come to focus almost exclusively on surgical or chemical techniques to effect cures, the need for methods to address long-term issues and the whole person has steadily grown with increasing human life spans. Because of growing, serious, even fatal resistance to drugs in many instances and the development of tolerance to pain-relieving medications, additional avenues are again being considered to bring relief from suffering. These methods include psychotherapy, herbal and homeopathic interventions, and multiple other approaches that work with the human energy system. Ultimately, the goal of all effective treatments is to prevent disease and future disabilities. Prevention through education of the public has again become a central focus in healthcare planning since treatment costs for long-term illnesses continue to spiral.

The current conventional medical model focuses on elimination of an illness by countering its effects on the body. The term *allopathic* describes this orientation, which aims to oppose the pathological disease process directly. For example, an infection is usually treated with an antibiotic, a substance that literally works *anti* (against) *bios* (life). This approach generally still works well for most acute conditions, and total eradication of the causative organism usually ensues. This is deemed a cure. Surgery also serves to remove the causative problem. As many are finding out, however, there are missing elements in these approaches. Patients may never learn how to prevent future infections or understand some of the many ways they can maintain high-level wellness. Because of its focus on separate symptoms rather than the whole person, mainstream healthcare in North America does not empower its consumers to become educated in natural and integrative ways to prevent or treat illness.

Other models of healthcare are becoming more prominent as public interest seeks enhanced well-being throughout the human life span. Initially, these approaches were labeled "alternative medicine." More recently, such approaches are called "complementary medicine," suggesting their function as a complement within an inclusive healthcare model.

The term "integrative healthcare" has come to the forefront to describe medical clinics and offices that acknowledge and encompass the best of both allopathic and complementary medicine. Integrative healthcare, thus, may involve conventional medical providers such as doctors, physician's assistants, and advanced registered nurse practitioners as well as counselors, herbalists, massage therapists, and energy medicine practitioners. The emphasis in integrative healthcare is not only on relief of symptoms but on client education and self-care. Healing, as differentiated from curing, deals with the whole person. Clients in integrative facilities learn from their pain and find ways to address underlying issues, to gain psychological insights about their stresses, to improve thought and belief patterns, to connect with their inner wisdom, and to honor and respect their unique humanity.

Current estimates are that more than 70 percent of the American population turns to one or more forms of complementary modalities to find physical and psychological relief.[1] This trend toward use of complementary modalities is significant, especially since most payments for services are not covered by insurers or Medicare and must be paid out of pocket.

Developments Toward Integrative Healthcare

A bit of history is helpful in understanding the evolution of the holistic, integrative thinking that supports the practice of energy therapies. The National Institutes of Health (NIH) has been the organizational bastion for conventional medical care in the United States. As a result of a consumer-led demand to legitimize other approaches in the 1980s, NIH established a small office of alternative (meaning nonallopathic) medicine. This office grew steadily and, by the beginning of the twenty-first century, a joint panel of leaders in conventional and holistic care practices decided the word "alternative" implied limited "either/or" choices to the patient. Use of the word "complementary" came into prominence, as it captured an approach that serves to fill out or complete conventional practices. Thus the National Center for Complementary and Alternative Medicine (NCCAM) was established to acknowledge, standardize, and initiate study of the diverse nonallopathic endeavors. NCCAM defined seven areas of these adjuncts to conventional medical care:[2]

1. Bioelectromagnetic applications.

2. Alternative systems of medical practice, including Oriental medicine, acupuncture, Ayurveda, homeopathy, and Native American medicine.

3. Manual healing methods, such as massage, somatic therapies, and chiropractic interventions.

4. Pharmacological and biological treatments not yet accepted by mainstream medicine, such as medical chelation.

5. Herbal medicines.

6. Treatments focusing on diet and nutrition in the prevention and treatment of chronic diseases.

7. Interventions that work with body and mind integration, such as yoga, prayer, mental healing, and energy medicine modalities.

The last category, energy medicine, is based on new understandings of the subtle energy and electromagnetic information system of the human body. Since some forms of this energy system cannot as yet be objectively measured, the discipline has been labeled "frontier medicine." The NCCAM budget is thin in comparison to the massive budgets for other NIH centers, such as the Center for the Study of Heart Disease, but it has been steadily gaining public interest since its inception. The inclusion of "energy modalities" as part of a national center is significant mainly because it acknowledges that our practices of energy modalities have an acknowledged place within complementary modalities and the larger framework of integrative healthcare.

Because energy medicine is such a newly emerging field, students and practitioners of energy modalities must take care to base their work on current knowledge and evidence-based practice. The Healing Touch Program, for example, is one of the leaders in energy medicine largely because of its careful attention to theory, scientific exploration, ongoing research, and the presence of viable, effective organizational and ethical structures. This kind of leadership is essential because well-known complementary legal advisor and healthcare ethicist Michael Cohen warns, "energy therapies still occupy a legal gray zone for many professions and in many states...."[3]

Because of the need for caution, each one of us practitioners needs to consider carefully our values, our ethical principles, and the standards that guide our professional endeavors. To function as a viable discipline within the healthcare field, it is imperative for each modality to describe clearly its underlying goals, code of behaviors, and accepted standards for practice. As yet, this is a long way off for most of the more than 250 existing programs of energy therapy. In her recent research, Linnie Thomas found only several dozen educational programs for energy practitioners that discuss practical ways of building and maintaining healthy relationships with clients. Even fewer have established codes of ethics and standards of practice that apply to client care, self-care, communication with other professionals, and awareness of legal issues related to their specific methods.[4]

National Organizations That Support CAM Concepts and Integrated Healthcare (IHC)

Several national organizations and educational resources seek to create the place for CAM (complementary and alternative medicine) within existing healthcare industries.[5] Each organization and its purpose is briefly described here:

1. National Academies within the Institute of Medicine

After several years of bringing CAM modalities to public awareness, the academies, in conjunction with the Institute of Medicine, convened a study committee in 2003 to explore scientific, policy, and practice questions that have arisen with the increased use of complementary methods. Study committees within the academies continue to identify major policy issues in four areas: the need for CAM research, the practices for CAM regulation in the United States and other countries, development of information flow between CAM and conventional medicine, and considerations regarding training and certification requirements. Their Summit on Integrative Healthcare in 2009 pointed the way to numerous elements of healthcare reform. Published proceedings from these and future meetings will have ongoing important impact on the use of energy-based methods within new models of healthcare. Their website is www.iom.edu.

2. **Integrated Healthcare Consortium, National Policy Dialogue to Advance IHC**

Another historic meeting that established communication among leaders in the nation's healthcare community to establish and develop integrated models was held in 2001 and set up ongoing recommendations to foster IHC, increase research allocations for health promotion, ensure widespread access to CAM and IHC in rural areas, achieve regulatory recognition for each professional group that wishes it, and ensure that CAM is effectively integrated into the Healthy People 2020 development and implementation. Reports are available at www.apma. net/federalaffairs-ihpc

3. **National Health Freedom Coalition (NHFC)**

The National Health Freedom Coalition is an organization dedicated to promoting access to all healthcare information, services, and treatments that people deem beneficial for their health and well-being. The organization plays a vital role in protecting the consumer's right to access practitioners of nonmainstream modalities such as energy medicine. Outdated laws in most states currently exist to restrict healing options for their residents—a situation that potentially leaves energy therapy practitioners legally vulnerable to charges of practicing medicine without a license. Access to dietary supplements, for example, is constantly at risk due to investigations by the Food and Drug Administration (FDA) and Federal Trade Commission (FTC) under these outdated laws. Laws that make the practice of nontraditional interventions grounds for disciplinary action for physicians are still on the books in most states and have dictated the narrow focus of established American healthcare at present.

NHFC works with its sister organization, National Health Freedom Action, to provide lobbying and to assist state health freedom groups in moving legislation that affords access to healthcare for all. With the help of these organizations, laws that protect consumer access to unlicensed healthcare providers have been passed in eight states: Oklahoma, Idaho, Minnesota, Rhode Island, California, Arizona, Louisiana, and New Mexico, while a number of other states, including Iowa, Montana, North Carolina, Ohio, Texas, Washington, and Wisconsin, are currently in the process of adding healthcare freedom legislation to their laws.[6]

The NHFC has also taken the health freedom movement worldwide with its "International Declaration of Health Freedom," which states, in part, that full access to healthcare practitioners, healers, researches, treatments, and services is an inherent and fundamental human right. This right should be independent of the actions of governments and regulatory public or private bodies. Their website is www.nationalhealthfreedom.org

4. Complementary and Alternative Medicine Blog

Attorney Michael H. Cohen publishes a blog that addresses many of the relevant legal, ethical, and regulatory issues associated with CAM, energy medicine, and integrative medicine. It is accessible via www.camlawblog.com. The information for discussion of practice risks and risk management given in the next chapter is based on this information. Readers are encouraged to update their understanding of CAM law frequently and also to seek local legal advice regarding setting up their practices.

The presence of national attention to CAM practices—which include our energy therapy endeavors—means that regulations, legislative maneuvers, and educational requirements that could impact our ability to practice will likely be considered and implemented. Energy medicine is as yet an unregulated field because it is so new and functioning largely under the radar of public awareness.

We also need to be realistic that there is growing opposition to CAM practices from mainstream medical practitioners. Some organizations, such as Quackwatch, are especially eager to debunk energy modalities. Their national website (www.quackwatch.com), run by physicians inimical to CAM, gives very biased information about energy therapies. Unfortunately, many mainstream healthcare professionals use information from such a website and remain unaware of the many reputable CAM practices.

Energy Modalities as a Needed Component in Today's Integrative Healthcare

Early in 2009, the first Summit on Integrative Medicine was held in Washington, DC, to initiate change in perspectives of healthcare toward increasing wellness through prevention. The trend toward integrative healthcare and primary prevention in medical care centers is unmistakable, with new healthcare legislation that has followed since then.

Healing Touch and Therapeutic Touch are modalities that are already vital components within the integrative healthcare movement. Because both are based on integrative, holistic principles derived from social sciences, the nursing process, and Dr. Jean Watson's internationally known theories of caring,[7] they have become aligned with existing models of care in medical institutions, outpatient care, hospice care, and home health. For hospitalized patients, practitioners of these modalities offer compassionate and intentional human caring from skilled professionals or trained volunteers to help alleviate pain, diminish pre- or post-procedural anxiety, and effect needed relaxation. In other medical facilities, such as the increasingly utilized one-day surgical centers and outpatient clinics, they often serve as the humanistic link to attend to patients' psychological needs in high-tech medical environments. In palliative or hospice settings, practitioners—who may be nurses, social workers, or lay volunteers—provide deeper levels of emotional and spiritual care to those suffering serious long-term illness and for those in the process of dying.

In many institutional settings, energy medicine practitioners are closely aligned with physicians and ancillary healthcare personnel as part of the full treatment team. In private care settings, which are attracting many energy practitioners, a wide variety of caregivers offer individualized energy-based treatments to address client issues. To increase their effectiveness, these practitioners also establish strong professional referral networks consisting of qualified specialists who bring needed and appropriate resources to their clients. For example, many clients come to energy medicine practitioners seeking alternative care because they have come to the limit of the conventional medical model, which says, in essence, "There is nothing more we can do for you." Worse, some clients come to believe that their symptoms are self-inflicted because of New Age misperceptions about the mind's power over the body. If they become ill, numerous patients believe they caused their illness in some way. Such people are often in need of medical care to manage pain or disability, and the energy-based practitioner can make referrals to holistically oriented providers, body workers, and related integrative healthcare practitioners.

Many energy medicine facilitators spontaneously uncover emotional trauma of which the client only had premonitions or was totally unaware. This can occur because trauma appears to be encoded in the body's neurological wiring as well as stored energetically in the biofield, its layers, meridians, and/or energy centers. Reliving of a traumatic experience can therefore surface spontaneously during a treatment session. Practitioners of energy methods can gently and successfully support those who have experienced trauma.

Our intention is always to assist client welfare by aligning with the unlimited supply of energy in the universe through the practitioner's centered focusing. This requires careful attention to our own needs and desires—from a place of personal well-being, as we'll explore later.

Models of Integrative Healthcare

Integrative healthcare models have already been studied and evaluated by American veterans administrations to find the best pathways for helping veterans with chronic pain, stress-related depression, and post-traumatic stress disorder (PTSD). A recent two-year study conducted in Salt Lake City, Utah, showed that their Integrative Health Clinic and Program effectively diminished patient symptoms without using extensive medication, instead focusing on psychological and sociological approaches.[8] Interest in helping veterans with complementary approaches is rapidly growing because of the complexity of problems that cannot be resolved with conventional medical care alone.

Another example of a dynamic integrative healthcare model is taking place at the Scripps Center for Integrative Medicine. Located near San Diego, California, the center offers instructional courses in a six-week program for coronary preventive care as well as for postcoronary recovery using the integrative medical model of well-known cardiologist Dr. Dean Ornish. The primary interventional cardiologist and leading nurse at the center are energy health practitioners who teach basic energetic interventions to the large numbers of patients enrolled in the program.

The integrative healthcare model with energy medicine involvement is also catching on in many other parts of the country. An example is the Cleveland Hospital in Ohio, which not only implemented energy modalities for its heart surgery patients, but also supported a fine research study regarding the role of energy medicine in helping patients' recovery after cardiac surgery. The study demonstrated many important effects of energy modalities and half a million dollars in savings to the hospital in reduced length of hospital stays.[9]

Many other models exist that combine conventional medical care with complementary modalities to provide an integrated practice for optimal patient benefit. A good example of a successfully operating integrative center is Whole Health Chicago.[10] The center is an independent medical clinic in which a large complement of practitioners united to formulate the best outcomes for their clients. The staff includes an internist physician, a chiropractor, an acupuncturist, a clinical psychologist specializing in energy psychology, a nutritionist, a homeopath, a massage therapist, an herbalist and flower essence expert, a physical therapist, and a Healing Touch practitioner. Psychologist Dr. Larry Stoler combines his clinical skills with expertise in energy psychology and medical qigong. The collaborative staff have worked together for nearly a decade to bring patients the best from both conventional allopathic medicine and complementary approaches.

The Importance of Professional Organizations

A professional organization establishes the value of a given modality. It can develop training and certification programs, develop research studies, and provide continuing education for its members. It can also be the resource for information and resources regarding practice issues that are likely to arise as increasing numbers of caregivers reach more clients.

Most significant, an organization can unite to defend its practitioners and to establish a particular modality as a viable, recognized practice. Please recall that most healing systems addressing the whole person are still regarded as on the fringe of accepted mainstream medical or psychological care. In addition, practitioners of energy therapies are as yet unable to demonstrate the exact mechanisms of healing actions, to define the absolute therapeutic value of their interventions, or to cite widespread acceptance from a critical mass of traditionally certified or licensed professionals. Another important consideration is that, from a legal standpoint, it is considered unethical to practice an innovative technique unless it has proven value and a great deal of evidence-based research.

Formal organizations demonstrate that a particular approach is effective for select clients and that the methods are valued by their members. Thus they provide a "defensible minority"—a known group that, by its existence, gives validity to a new approach or modality. In contrast, complementary modalities that do not have the benefit of national or state organizations run the risk of being subject to regulations from outside agencies that may seek to limit or actually ban the practice of a particular methodology.

A professional organization can also identify its foundational values, ethical principles, and practice standards. By doing so, members of the organization are in a better position to defend their methods if questioned by regulatory agencies or the legal system.

Creating standards for practice is important because when something is written it gains credibility and begins to shape the way practitioners think and behave. Writing professional standards as outlined and discussed in this book can reflect the values of the organization and its practitioners. Publishing and disseminating the information reminds members and public constituents about the integrity of the work and the vision of the organization. (Major organizations who support energy practitioners are listed in appendix C).

* * * *

As elaborated in this chapter, there are many resources available to energy therapy practitioners through the growing national networks of NCCAM as well as organizations that function to assist energy modality practitioners. We are interconnected with other practitioners within CAM as a whole. The new field of energy medicine benefits greatly from these connections because other practitioners have helped to pave the paths that bring credibility to our individual endeavors.

We turn now to explore the reality of legal requirements for anyone who establishes a practice for the public and to consider the essentials of risk management that must be part of every practitioner's consciousness.

CHAPTER THREE

LEGAL CONSIDERATIONS AND RISK MANAGEMENT

O f the more than 250 currently active programs of energy therapies that author Linnie Thomas researched for *The Encyclopedia of Energy Medicine*,[1] sixty-five were selected for inclusion and given in-depth descriptions. The selection criteria for inclusion in the book were evidence of professionalism, longevity, and diversity. Staying power and ability to reach wide audiences is generally indicative of organizational planning and professional integrity. Even within these parameters, however, fewer than thirty of the modalities selected for the encyclopedia had stated codes of ethics or professional standards of practice.

Given the trend toward retaining outdated thinking and laws, as described in the previous chapter, a viable practice of an energy modality must include awareness of national and local laws, and hold to professional standards in its practice. Participation in an organization that can support and validate its practitioners is also essential. Energy therapy practitioners are pioneers in work that is innovative and novel and also still in early experimental stages of development. Knowing our place within the CAM structure, interfacing with the regulatory agencies that help to shape the future of healthcare, working toward acceptance from mainstream healthcare, understanding risks, and knowing the best ways to engage in risk management—all these are essentials for negotiating a personal career in our new field.

Thus we begin with a brief overview of legal considerations and the most basic professional standards before moving on to specific energetic concepts that will help us to build healing, appropriate, and right relationships with ourselves, our clients, and our communities.

Legal Principles

Practitioners of energy therapies adhere to the legal guidelines developed by the professional license under which they practice. Unlicensed practitioners of energy therapies hold themselves to the recently established legal principle of what a reasonable person with a similar background and in a similar situation would do, known as the "duty of due care."

Related Standards of Practice

- Licensed energy therapy practitioners (ETPs) are familiar with and conduct themselves within the codes of ethics and professional standards of their publicly sanctioned profession.

- Violation of the codes and standards of one's profession automatically becomes a violation of one's practice in a stated energy modality.

- Unlicensed ETPs hold themselves to the standard of care in keeping with their highest personal values, their preeminent regard for client welfare, and their understanding of how a reasonable person in a similar situation would act.

- Both licensed and unlicensed ETPs seek immediate help and guidance regarding any practice dilemma that may arise in the performance of their professional activities.

- Both licensed and unlicensed ETPs know and understand the need to adhere to professional standards in their use of energy modalities and make every effort to avoid legal liabilities in their practices.

- Both licensed and unlicensed ETPs implement risk management practices rigorously.

Potential Liability Risks in the Practice of Energy Therapies

Because our field is new and not yet well defined, there are a number of risks into which the unaware practitioner may stumble. Fortunately, most can be prevented with reasonable cautionary steps. Here are some of the predominant practice risks I've noted over the past twenty years of teaching energy methods to practitioners and of giving consultation regarding standards of care to colleagues, professionals, and organizations linked to energy therapies:

- Offering clients a modality, such as energy therapy, that has as-yet limited evidence for safety or effectiveness without giving backup information from current medical literature, research, and peer-reviewed professional journals.

- Failure to know a client's medical issues; failure to confirm the presence of adequate medical care; failure to know the client's medications or use of vitamins or supplements.

- Recommending or selling supplements, medicines, or devices within one's practice (unless you are a licensed medical provider).

- Failure to use a robust process of informed consent that includes dialogue with the client about a procedure or approach to be used, obtaining client permission, and respecting client choice.

- Financial impropriety, such as fee-splitting when making a referral, or other forms of profit-sharing.

- Making claims in marketing materials, including website, brochures, publicity, or public presentations, that are inconsistent with

FDA (Food and Drug Administration) and FTC (Federal Trade Commission) guidelines.

- Promising more than you can deliver within your current skill level.

- Neglecting to have a current business license in the community in which you have set up your practice.

Best Risk Management Practices

The best ways to avoid risk of liability and legal entanglements is, logically, to implement a risk management strategy that counters and avoids such risky behaviors. Here's a quick overview of the basic elements:

- Since energy therapies are so new, evaluating the literature, theory, and research is essential in order to know the safety and efficacy of any approach you are using.

- Keep backup files of the literature and research that you have studied and that can be used to educate your clients as needed. There is plenty of research evidence now available to support energetic approaches and you need to be current in knowing and explaining your method's scientific base.

- Provide clear informed consent to your clients based on your specific practice that takes into account knowledge of risks and benefits of the approaches you're using. Document the fact that you have discussed your method's procedures and that the client has given permission freely, without coercion. Check in frequently with clients to make sure they are still consciously choosing the approaches you are employing.

- Continue to support client's conventional diagnostic and therapeutic regimens, monitor any new symptoms, and make sure they are carefully evaluated. Document your knowledge of the client's medical issues and confirmation that adequate care is being provided.

- Seek consultation for complex client issues that are beyond your skill level to handle effectively.

- Refer to appropriate practitioners for client needs that are outside your scope of practice.

- Develop and maintain clear, professional, therapeutically oriented agreements with clients. (Specific hints: don't sell things to your clients, coerce them to attend programs, make deals, or drive them in your car.)

- Seek legal consultation on all publicity about yourself and your practice.

- Maintain a current business license in your locality and seek legal counsel to make sure your practice functions within accepted legal parameters.

The effective risk reduction recommendations given here will be developed further as we proceed in this book and look at client care from an energy therapy perspective.

Legal Hazards for Both
Unlicensed and Licensed Energy Professionals

Informal sharing of energy therapies can happen briefly with friends or neighbors, but whenever you are engaged in an endeavor that is available to the public, includes any form of advertising or publicity, or has a marketable value, you are functioning as a professional practitioner. Thus, even if you are not licensed in a legally sanctioned profession, such as nursing, social work, or counseling, you are still open to legal liabilities in relation to your actions. You may unwittingly step into scope-of-practice issues, possible malpractice or negligence, or possible misrepresentation of yourself that could be interpreted as fraud or violation of confidentiality. Alternately, you could be accused of assault and battery for improper touching.

State statutes, regulations, licensing boards, and legally interpreted cases define the scope of practice and standards of licensed professionals. Unlicensed practitioners are not subject to such rules and, therefore, don't have the protection of an identified profession. In some ways, unlicensed practitioners are thus more vulnerable to potential legal action. For example, giving in-depth counseling that is the purview of a licensed profession could be considered a criminal act of practicing counseling without the appropriate license or education. Although healthcare freedom legislation (as mentioned in chapter 2) lessens this exposure in some states, unlicensed practitioners must tread very carefully in the conduct of their practices.

The two most frequent areas of legal liability are *malpractice*, when the practitioner undertakes an action that is deemed harmful to the client, and *negligence*, when a practitioner fails the "duty of due care," which results in a form of harm to a client.[2] Courts will attempt to determine in either case whether the practitioner acted in a way that a "reasonable practitioner" within a similar modality would act.

Inadequate informed consent from the client is a major potential area for negligence by practitioners. Informed consent implies the client knows what the practitioner will do and possible outcomes of the treatment. In assessing whether a specific failure to disclose information of a method has violated the informed consent obligation, courts will seek to identify whether a reasonable patient would find the information that was given sufficient to make an educated decision to agree to or refuse a treatment. (Further discussions of informed consent are in chapter 8 and a sample form is in appendix B).

Fraud and misrepresentation involve knowingly relying on inaccurate or false information for personal benefit or to the detriment of the client.[3] Recklessly failing to discover if information is true or false in the trusted position of being a practitioner can open you to possible claims of fraud by clients. Fraud is harder to prove than negligence, since intention and recklessness have to be proven. Fraud is, therefore, a less likely charge.

Confidentiality is the ongoing obligation of caregivers to keep private the client information shared with them *during* and *after* the course of treatment. This obligation exists until the client grants permission for it to be breached or a situation arises that falls within one of the exceptions to confidentiality (described further in chapter 8). Having clients sign a release of information form, which grants the practitioner permission to speak to a related healthcare professional for purpose of optimizing the plan of care, is the accepted method for discussing client needs among professionals. State and federal statutes, including the Health Insurance Portability and Accountability Act (HIPAA) have increased requirements for such signed releases. HIPAA is the formal law passed in 1996 that encompasses prior less formal protections of clients' medical information.

Exceptions to confidentiality include an extreme client emergency, a written waiver that gives permission to release specific information, or the possibility that the client may be in imminent danger of harming self or others. Even with these exceptions, confidentiality should be breached only to the least extent needed to accomplish the necessary goal. Practitioners may also have a duty to breach confidentiality under law in some states when it is necessary to protect a third party from potential violence or other risks posed by the client, such as carrying an infection or genetic predisposition to serious disease.[4] States vary in specific legal requirements for practitioners to report abuse of children and/or elders and the parameters of duty to warn, so be sure to know your state's regulations concerning client confidentiality and abuse reporting laws.

Assault and battery is another potential legal liability. Assault is defined in legal terms as "creating an imminent apprehension of harm" but may include verbal threats or making threatening gestures. Battery is physical contact without consent. Physical contact that is not condoned with express client permission in a therapeutic setting could be construed as possible sexual misconduct. Increasingly, failure to obtain consent for physical contact is deemed to be a form of negligence.

The Resources of the Professional Organization

A professional organization with research information, educational and certification programs, and internal codes of ethics and standards of practice is a credible witness and can fulfill the evolving legal theory called the "respectable minority defense." Courts and licensing boards could accept expert testimony regarding innovative methods, even though they are not yet fully accepted in mainstream healthcare, if they are supported by significant research and used responsibly according to standards set by the organization.

VIGNETTES FOR SECTION I

Vignette I.1 Assuming Clients Are Willing

A dentist in a northern state was ordered to appear in front of her licensing board to respond to complaints from six patients. The major complaint was that the dentist administered energy modalities without explanation to her patients while doing dental procedures. She had learned these techniques at a weekend workshop. Patients felt they did not get the information needed to grant permission or to make an educated choice. Further, there was no documentation to show they had received any information about the dentist's "new procedures."

Each state board regulates the practice of dentistry, and energy modalities are not considered part of standard dental practice. In addition to charges of not obtaining informed consent, the particular board brought up charges of violating the professional standard for documentation, for practicing below the standard of care for the dental profession, and obligating patients to purchase supplements.

Apparently, the dentist did not consider her patients to be partners in decision-making. Additionally, the action taken did not appear to be in service of specific patient needs but, rather, met the practitioner's desire for practicing what she had learned. By failing to consider patients' rights of choice and by assuming agreement, the dentist misused the power differential inherent in the therapeutic relationship.

Discussion: Until recently, energy modalities were generally considered noninvasive and to have no side effects other than relaxation. Actually, there is a great deal of communication that occurs via the interacting energy fields of client and practitioner. There are also possible risks in the use of energy modalities, as we'll explore later. In today's world of expanded privacy laws and patient rights, informed consent is an essential component of any treatment approach.

Vignette I.2

Client Chooses Not to Receive More Energy Interventions

Bert heard a lot of good things about Joy, the new energy practitioner in his community. He really had no idea what would be involved and was surprised at the careful and knowledgeable explanation Joy gave him. He wanted to "get fixed" for his memory lapses and scattered thinking.

As she discussed treatment plans further, Joy noted that Bert talked incessantly and also had some attentional deficits. Joy gave Bert some exercises to balance his energy field. Though he said he liked the exercises, Bert said he did not want to do any of the suggested homework to help himself.

Joy followed the plan they agreed to in the session and Bert liked her attentions. But when it came to making a return appointment, Bert declined, stating he did not realize he had to participate actively in the treatment.

They parted on positive terms, leaving the door open to further learning if Bert so chose at a later time. Joy documented the informed consent steps she had gone through, the exercises discussed and given, and the client's choice. She closed the file with the sense that she had done the best she could and that the single session might prompt Bert to seek other forms of care in the future.

Discussion: Not all clients find energy therapies to be a good fit, despite their high expectations and stated desires. Accepting the client's choice may be difficult, especially at the beginning of one's practice, but the goal of caregiving is met when the invitation remains open for further meetings or exploration.

* * * *

Energy healing practices may be highly individualistic, but they operate within the context of municipal requirements, regional regulations, and national legal structures. Careful understanding of the areas discussed in this chapter will lend credibility to you as a practitioner and to the entire emerging discipline of energy therapies. As caring professionals, we have every reason to utilize available resources, such as professional consultation and making referrals, to maximize outcome for our clients and to minimize personal risks.

We proceed now to exploring the practitioner's preparation for energy therapy endeavors, specific issues in relationships to clients, and the development of one's practice within a community.

SECTION II:

WALKING YOUR TALK– STANDARDS FOR ESTABLISHING AND MAINTAINING A HEALTHY, HEALING RELATIONSHIP WITH YOURSELF AS A PRACTITIONER

We have to treat ourselves with loving-kindness and equanimity, gentleness, and dignity before we can accept, respect, and care for others…
—theoretician of the caring-healing model Dr. Jean Watson

Ethical Principles:

Practitioners of energy therapies maintain the integrity and balance of their personal energy systems. They commit to ongoing self-awareness and seek counseling and consultation resources to resolve their internal challenges or conflicts.

Related Standards of Practice:

- Energy therapy practitioners (ETPs) seek consciously to increase their awareness of their own issues related to physical, emotional, mental, and spiritual needs and vulnerabilities.

- ETPs administer self-care for personal needs as soon as they become aware of personal disturbances or uneasiness and readily seek appropriate external resources for themselves.

- ETPs trust their knowing and inner wisdom and commit to careful thinking to avoid overinvolvement, dependence, or undue attachments to any one person's point of view.

- ETPs actively seek additional learning opportunities to increase their skills and for their personal development.

- ETPs prepare themselves carefully before each client sessions and strive to maintain the health of their own energy systems.

- ETPs set caring intention for their clients' highest good and release personal attachments to outcomes.

- ETPs are aware of their own vulnerabilities that may arise in client relationships and seek resolution of conflicts as soon as possible.

Chapter Four

Why Care of Self Is Primary

Since all movement toward wholeness and health really comes from within each individual, caregivers must know how to provide effective care for themselves as a priority. Gone are the days when it was believed that helping professionals must put the needs of others first. The most effective of today's caregivers have learned they must establish a right, purposeful relationship with themselves before attempting to reach out to those in need. This is not only a good idea—it is essential, particularly in the practice of energy therapies.

Although there are now over two hundred educational programs for specific energy therapies, ranging in length from two weekends to four years, my experience in consulting with energy-linked practitioners is that, in almost all programs, far too little attention is given to personal care. It is as if there is a blind spot in our vision: we often lack the insights that allow us to appreciate and know the person most immediately entrusted to our care—one's very own self.

The reality of biofield interactions is one of the most valued aspects of energy therapies. Interaction with the caregiver's balanced, integrated field appears to help clients shift toward higher vibrational patterns, to gain better understanding of themselves, and to generate personal insights. As many practitioners will attest, energy therapy goes far beyond mere words—something magical happens when we understand our interactions with clients from the perspective of interacting energy fields.

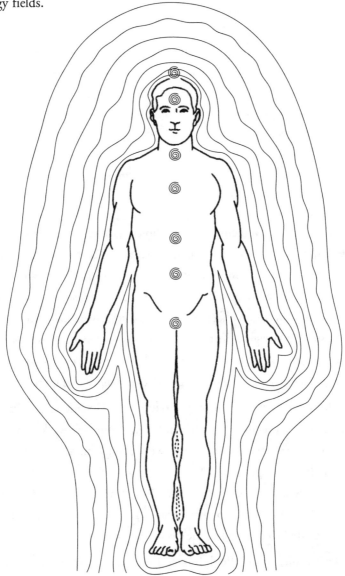

Illustration 4.1 – The Human Biofield and Related Chakras

Illustration 4.2 – Sample Image of Interactive Biofields—
Practitioner and Client

Here are some of the most powerful reasons for seeing practitioner self-care as a central professional standard for the practice of energy therapies:

- Active attention to self-care empowers the practitioner to be fully present to the client by bringing caring intention into clear focus.

- Self-care is essential in preventing practitioner burnout.

- Knowledge of one's strengths and weaknesses permits honest, objective, and compassionate awareness of the humanity of others.

- Balance of the caregiver's personal energy system permits unobstructed flow from the infinite supply of energy in the universe to the client.

Let's discuss each of these aspects in turn.

Self-Care as the Gateway to Being Fully Present to Clients

In the movie *ET,* the lost extraterrestrial receives an essential message that tells him to connect with his home base so he can get reoriented and return to his galaxy. "ET phone home" has become a catch phrase that has permeated our everyday language ever since. Touching home base is not only a good practice for adventuresome adolescents who need to check in with their parents, but also a message to all who need to reorient themselves to their sense of purpose. Whatever our dilemmas are, the connection with inner wisdom is nurtured by establishing a sense of calm and peacefulness. The human body appears to be wired with its own homing device that reminds us to return to center and "reboot" our minds.

Reconnecting to one's own center with mindful awareness is both an easy and challenging endeavor. Although techniques for centering are easily learned, it takes most practitioners a lifetime of practice to be able to access their own center quickly when it's most needed. Mindful awareness and presence enhances the ability of the mind to focus so you can help yourself as well as others in need.

Think of a recent situation when you felt overwhelmed by life. Misplacing a needed object, having a flat tire when in a hurry, getting a costly traffic ticket, losing your precious material into the unknown belly of the computer, receiving a troubling medical diagnosis, hearing about a loved one's distress, learning of another major environmental disaster— these are just a sampling of events that can move most people off center. Returning to "home base" reestablishes connection with the place of steady assurance and a sense of confidence that things can work out in a positive way. In truth, it does not take much for most people to lose their bearings and become "unglued." Without being overly pessimistic, it is a truism that anything can happen to anyone at any time. Life *is* both precarious and precious. And it's wise to be prepared to expect the unexpected.

Here is a mindful awareness practice that is taught in some form in almost all energy therapies as a preparation for the practitioner. In addition, taking time to center allows the caregiver to set clear intention toward the highest good for the client prior to giving an energetic intervention.

Exercise 4.1 Sample Centering Practice

- Wherever you are, just before meeting a client, set aside five to ten minutes for establishing your own energy balance.

- Take a deep breath and release it fully, as if blowing out a candle.

- Repeat taking in the breath and make sure you release pressures and tensions from the body fully with each out-breath.

- Resume your normal breathing rhythm, while sending warmth and caring to any part of the body that feels tight or constricted.

- See your whole body surrounded and interpenetrated by the energy of nature and the universe around you.

- Feel warmth and aliveness in your heart and let this quality of energy flow into your arms, to the palms of your hands.

- Allow a thought or image to come to you to symbolize your intention for the person with whom you will be working.

- While continuing to feel your inner peace and support of the universal energies, move into connecting with your client. Notice how easily you can be fully present to the person you meet.

Centering practices may take less time with experience, but the conscious setting of one's caring intention and releasing personal issues are always necessary. Professional energy healing sessions should flow easily without any sense of being drained or stressed. Centering after a session is also recommended to release any tension or burdens you may have inadvertently picked up from interacting with the client's biofield.

Taking on client issues in any way or feeling burdened suggests that mindful awareness is missing in some way. Research shows that practitioners who regularly practice centered awareness actually live longer and with better health than other healthcare professionals.[1] Practitioners who draw from their own ego strengths or physical resources are more prone to suffering energetic depletions. They may become bored or frustrated with their enterprise; some even drop out of healing endeavors altogether.

Connecting with one's inner being and the energetic resources of nature is, therefore, a hallmark of the professional practice of energy therapists.

Prevention of Burnout

Education about what is called compassion fatigue or burnout is still in its infancy. However, its symptoms, such as exhaustion, preoccupation with being busy, losing one's sense of purpose and direction, and overwhelming discouragement, have become recognized as some of the greatest risk factors in all professions that address human distress. This would include not only hospital-based personnel, but also firefighters, EMTs, police officers, rescue workers, volunteer caregivers and, for our purposes in this book, practitioners of energy therapies.

Strong examples of burnout or compassion fatigue abounded in news reports about emergency personnel in the World Trade Center disaster of September 11, 2001. Severe fatigue and despair resulted not only from the attack, the chaotic loss of lives, and the trauma's immediate aftermath, but also from finding so few people to actually help. The highly charged desire to help and save lives was thwarted when survivors became increasingly difficult to find. Everybody, including the uninjured, was in a state of shock. Many emergency personnel continued with feelings of hopelessness and helplessness, suffering deepening emotional depression, for months and even years later. Even the rescue dogs on the disaster scene started moping about and becoming listless. Creative search and rescue personnel set up staged situations so that the dogs could uncover a live person in the debris. The trained canines could then feel the satisfaction of success and released cheerful yelps. Their enthusiasm helped to dispel the intense gloom.

Although there is a growing body of literature and research to confirm the reality of compassion fatigue, popularly known as burnout, and its many symptoms, few medical or social service programs actually teach ways of preventing or treating its effects.[2] The nursing profession is at the forefront of human caring by responding to immediate distress in hospital and outpatient settings. It has been perhaps most visibly affected by caregiver burnout and compassion fatigue. New graduates often leave the profession within just one to two years after graduation or find less demanding jobs.[3] Some leave institutional careers to go into other branches of human relations work and, understandably, many seek well-known energy healing practices, such as Healing Touch and Therapeutic Touch. These established practices, which began within nursing, allow healthcare workers to reclaim their wish to alleviate human suffering directly within the high-tech, mechanized world of modern medicine.

Part of caregiver burnout relates to hearing the distressing stories of clients and survivors of profound trauma. Thus, energy health practitioners are additionally at high risk for what is now called "vicarious traumatization"—the indirect trauma of experiencing a client's pain or life situation. As practitioners, we know well how to treat energy imbalance in our clients, but we may forget to identify our own need for relief from exposure to others' trauma. Knowing when your own energy system is out of balance is a helpful place to begin. It may spur you to self-treatment with the very energy modalities you enjoy teaching to others.

Exercise 4.2 Sample Self-Assessment of Personal Energies

Rate the following statements by asking yourself how often you think or act on each: never, hardly ever, sometimes, quite often, or always.

1. I like being on time.

2. I have difficulty being on time.

3. I frequently have to rush to get somewhere.

4. Except for occasional emergencies, I'm in charge of my schedule.

5. I set high expectations for myself.

6. I meet most expectations of myself and feel satisfied with my progress.

7. At the end of the day, it seems I've never done enough.

8. When I have a strong emotion, I take time to process it and learn about myself.

9. I make critical comments to myself.

10. I take time daily to exercise, play, and do what gives me pleasure.

11. Some days, there is just not enough time for my needs.

12. I like to sit still and let images, associations, and new ideas come to me.

You may notice that items 2, 3, 5, 7, 9, and 11 indicate a need for more caution toward yourself. Presence of these patterns in your life can be the beginning of burnout even in the fascinating career you've chosen.

Using the energy exercises you know may be a good starting place. Seeking professionals who can nurture your being is also at the heart of successful burnout prevention. I strongly suggest receiving massage on a regular basis, engaging in preventative medical and dental care, seeking sound nutritional advice, and getting plenty of restorative sleep. Consulting with a counselor or mentor to be your "soul friend" when you feel an emotional deficit or especially thorny issue is a mark of good mental health and a highly valued standard for energy therapy practitioners.[4]

Self-Knowledge Enhances Compassion for Others

Another dimension of self-care is honest and objective self-appraisal. This does not have to be expressed as criticism; rather, it is a healthy practice of being objective about oneself and progressing toward enhanced consciousness. One exercise that many enjoy is simply to identify strengths and areas for further development. You may wish to do this for yourself.

Here's a sampling from the notebook of an energy practitioner with whom I consulted recently.

Personal Strengths	Areas for Further Development
Heartfelt enthusiasm for helping people in need	Being able to step back and not take on client issues
Strong interest in facilitating client pain relief	Expanding knowledge of pain pathways, physiology of pain, and learning additional pain relief methods
Self-confident and assertive	Ability to listen with more attention to client nuances

As can be seen, each strength also holds seed material for further development of one's skills and personal strengths. As your compassion toward self unfolds, compassion for those who suffer physical or emotional distress also expands.

A highly valued standard of professional practice is to seek feedback about oneself, to be willing to learn more about one's chosen field, and to strive continually for better understanding and personal improvement.

"Know thyself" was Plato's wisdom that summarized the humanistic philosophy of ancient Greece more than 2,500 years ago. This people-centered tradition is still apparent in the many forms of recognition our society gives to people who not only have intelligence, but who also use their gifts to help others. Sharing energy therapies is one of the most humane endeavors anyone can offer and, with it, we have ready opportunity to engage in deepening self-insight.

Human assets and follies are readily transparent when clients reveal themselves to us. Our preparation, learning, centered awareness, and striving to become more fully ourselves permits clients to sense our commitment to personal growth. Even the most disturbed client can feel when the practitioner comes from a place of emotional integrity.

A Balanced Energy System Reduces Obstructions to Seeing Clients Objectively

Outer layers of the practitioner's energy sheath or field are easily sensed by clients because many of them are already highly sensitive to vibrational emanations. The quality of the practitioner's energy system streams forth from the depth of inner work that has been done.

Our energies become the lens through which we see our clients. If a practitioner has personal issues that cannot be set aside with centering and preparation, her vision of the client may be compromised or limited. If a practitioner is caught in believing that client dependency is a good attribute, he may inadvertently transfer that consciousness to a needy person. If the helper holds a victim consciousness, she may see the victimization of her client and ignore his strengths.

Distortions can therefore abound if therapists do not have a healthy relationships—and resultant balanced energy system—with themselves. One of the most noticeable dangers is the dynamic of projection, which assumes that whatever the practitioner senses or sees is actually true for the client.

Psychological literature abounds with examples of psychotherapists who make conscious and unconscious assumptions about their clients based on their own projections and possible desires for fame. One of the most disturbing projections pattern has been described as "false memory syndrome."[5] Because some counselors were overeager to uncover childhood abuse, they assumed, on the basis of very thin evidence, that many of their clients had been molested in childhood. Further, they assumed legal retribution would help the clients. The resulting mayhem created great distress to the accused, the clients themselves, and the entire legal field. Healing is usually not served in courts of justice, where the emotional needs of clients are frequently ignored or trampled. Reporting of genuine—not assumed—abuse is, of course, a legal requirement, as discussed in the previous chapter. Related considerations will be discussed later, as we look at client and community relationships.

Needless to say, a healthy relationship with oneself is requisite when you are in the empowered position of being the caregiver. Clients all too easily assume the practitioner is correct in making his or her projections or suggestions. This becomes even more complex when we consider the use of intuition, which is also emphasized in many energy therapy practices.

Many Native American traditions hold that we cannot understand other people's needs until we've actually experienced their situation or "walked in their moccasins." Healthy relations within foster deep respect for whatever clients may be experiencing. Your best resource as a practitioner is to "walk your talk"—be the best person you can be through inner work and ongoing dedication to self-reflection.

CHAPTER FIVE

LEARNING FROM PERSONAL INTERFERENCES

That which we do not bring into consciousness
appears in our lives as fate.
—Carl Gustav Jung, leading psychologist of the unconscious mind

cknowledging our humanity as practitioners is sometimes humbling. But humility helps us to recognize that the best intentions are often not enough to meet the complex needs of our clients. Beyond legal requirements, which attempt to regulate the worst practitioner misdemeanors, there is the large domain of ethical values and practice considerations that have no easy answers. Most client-caregiver relationships have gray areas, aspects that cannot be clearly delineated by thinking in terms of right or wrong, black or white.

To negotiate these entangled territories, practitioners need to be aware of their personal blocks, distortions, or impediments that may limit clear thinking and objectivity. The caregiver's energy system is like a lens through which he or she sees and interprets the world. If the lens is foggy or has a flaw, like past glitches in the Hubble space telescope, one cannot see with clarity: huge areas may be obscured or distorted. If we have good self-insight and release accumulated tensions on a daily basis, we are much more likely to be unobstructed channels for our clients. We will also be able to differentiate client issues from our own material—an essential skill in working with intuitive knowing that we'll discuss in chapter 7.

Doing therapeutic personal work thus opens the pathways for energy—our *qi*—to flow readily. Regular "energy hygiene" empowers our core values so they are conscious and available in difficult times and to make meaningful choices. It allows our vitality to flow to others and bring them hope and encouragement.

The profiles and statistics from a number of state licensing boards show that practitioner overconfidence is a major factor in client complaints and possible lawsuits. Thinking they know the answers, many practitioners miss important client cues or take on responsibilities that exceed their skills and knowledge. Overestimation of one's competence and lack of listening skills and inner attunement appear to be basic traits in some Western cultures. The extensive sociological research of Kruger and Dunning[1] demonstrated that mindsets made prior to an encounter with a problem or challenge persuaded advocates to take actions that they believed would be helpful rather than seeking those that fit the issue at hand. The divergence between client need and caregiver opinion becomes exacerbated in the presence of arrogance, rigidity, and self-righteousness.

In this chapter, we'll explore how distortions in the caregiver's energies can interfere with making accurate discernments. We'll also consider the many energetic ways practitioner flexibilities can be enhanced to prevent future distress.

Identifying Personal Interferences and Energetic Blockages

Transference

The psychological term "transference" is used as shorthand to describe the intricate process by which clients and practitioners establish relatedness. In energy therapies, rapid and deep rapport is the norm as the two interacting biofields begin to mesh. Positive transference is enhanced when the caregiver sets clear and respectful boundaries at the outset regarding fees, time of service, place of meeting, confidentiality, frequency of contact, choices, and permissions. Willingness of the client to follow the helper's gestures, humor, train of thought, or suggestions is a sign of positive transference and can frequently be noted early in first meetings.

The relationship between caregiver and client in energy therapies is often much more intense than that found in cognitive talk therapies or in medically oriented settings. Clients' rationalizations, defenses, or entangled thinking patterns are not operant when the basis of treatment is energetic attunement and intervention. Instead, the healing interaction is marked by deep rapport and trust, which allows clients to access their inner resources.

Client expectations for energy treatments may far exceed what the helper can realistically give. Thus, transference can lead to the assumption that the caregiver can magically transform one's entire life. While this may be flattering to the novice, it creates an unfortunate situation for both parties. Client trust has to be built on realistic and openly discussed expectations that can direct and focus ongoing interactions.

Another aspect of transference and rapid rapport is the implied responsibility for the caregiver to be genuine and honest in the relationship. Being entrusted with the care of another person's physical, psychological, and spiritual needs puts the burden of proof on the practitioner to guide the interaction toward positive outcomes. It is temptingly easy to allow the nature of transference to foster false dependencies on the practitioner for comfortable, long-term relationships. Client self-reliance, insight, and efficacy are the most desirable and worthy goals of any energy healing treatment process.

Countertransference

Another well-used psychological term, "countertransference," describes the caregiver's nonobjective reaction to the client based on the caregiver's personal history. For example, the client may come to be seen as a victim of life circumstances because the helper as suffered a similar unresolved situation. At times, a client's issues resonate with a caregiver's needs in such a way as to obstruct the ability to set a healthy, therapeutic direction. Take, for example, a client who is quite childlike and frequently asks the practitioner's opinion for advice. Wanting to be helpful, the helper unwittingly falls into the trap of giving solutions and acting like a parent instead of facilitating the client's personal work. Over time, the dependency patterns often increase and begin to burden the caregiver with frequent demands. An even worse outcome would be the client's blaming the practitioner if the advice given does not pan out, which can lead to negative gossip or even legal actions.

More advanced cases of countertransference may become evident when the practitioner actually dislikes the client for some reason and dreads seeing her again. If the practitioner accepts this inner distress and becomes attuned to it, he can make a conscious choice to heal those issues within himself. The client is then experienced as a much different person and compassion and empathy for the client can develop.

Feeling overwhelmed with client issues is another well-known sign of overinvolvement by caregivers. Often, consultation is needed to extricate from the complexities of such enmeshed client-practitioner relationships. The best prevention is to be exacting about treatment plans and goals with your clients at the outset and to maintain the boundaries that you both set and discuss.

Attachments

Another well-identified caregiver obstruction is having strong personal attachments to specific client outcomes. All people need financial security, including practitioners, but continuing to see a client who may actually benefit more from another form of treatment indicates unhealthy attachment. Hanging onto client relationships to meet one's own emotional needs would be another pitfall. Being disappointed when clients choose different goals than those the caregiver considers best might be evidence of an attachment to one's power. Practitioner desire to be right or controlling moves the whole relationship away from focus on client needs.

The prescription for resolving attachments in their many forms is relatively simple:

- Recognize when your goal is more important than the client's.

- Recognize when it seems that you are working harder than the client.

- Identify what specifically you hope to accomplish in your time with the client.

- Release whatever interferes with your and the client's genuine purpose and intention.

- Reconsider your goals and actions in light of the higher good of the client and the mutually agreed-upon goals.

- Learn all you can from each situation through careful self-examination and personal journaling.

Codependency

Frequently, caregivers overextend themselves to the point of physical or emotional detriment. This is called codependence. Helpers may not recognize the actual toll of listening to client issues without respite for themselves. They may become drained energetically without recognizing the early signs of burnout. The revealing book *I'm Dying to Take Care of You* addresses the high levels of codependence among medical caregivers and the effects of this pattern on one's health.[2]

Noting when we are overextended, modifying overwhelming schedules, mitigating personal stresses, resetting self-expectations, making sure we give care to body, mind, and spirit—these are some of the most practical ways to counteract tendencies toward codependency. Solid, healthy relationships with all parts of ourselves—including the unlovely ones—are needed in order to be effective in guiding others.

Personal Shadow Material

As mentioned, each practitioner's personality includes darker, hidden sides along with the healing light we want to shine on others. The great psychologist Carl Gustav Jung coined the term "human shadow" to describe the unconscious parts of ourselves that may emerge unexpectedly when we are under pressure or feeling stressed. Our feelings and behaviors at certain times are a puzzle: sometimes we are a mystery to ourselves.

Because shadow material is generally so elusive and different from our desired self-perceptions, it is difficult to track. One way of discovering this part of yourself is to think of the qualities or traits you most dislike in others. For example, if you have strong aversions to someone's being late, you may have difficulty with punctuality yourself or you may secretly dislike your own lack of organization. When you have adverse reactions to people who complain a lot, who avoid conflicts, find fault, blame others, or hate messes, you may, in fact, be holding onto a part of you that is perfectionistic and does not like to acknowledge those all-too-human traits within you. Most people want to reject certain qualities in others because they are too well known within themselves. Of course, all issues are much easier to see in others. Once we grasp the idea that these realities have something to do with us, we can begin to reclaim our power. We may be able to laugh a bit or confess without pain, "Hmm, I know something about that trait also."

Abraham Lincoln was a man of great wisdom who had good knowledge of his shadow traits and could therefore appeal to the higher good in each person he met. He acknowledged his shadow side readily; in psychological terms, we would say he had "eaten his shadow" by integrating and understanding it. When a lady complained on the campaign trail in 1860 that he was too ugly to be president, he replied with equanimity, "Yes, madam, and what would you like me to do about it?"

By acknowledging the shadow, the energy that was consumed in maintaining denial of less flattering personal attributes can be transformed into the energy of increased self-awareness, spontaneity, humor, and ability to laugh at personal flaws. Interestingly, as we learn to accept shadow parts of ourselves, we generate increased tolerance for the mistakes of others. It is easier to accept others as they really are, not as we want them to be.

Developing Personal Energy Hygiene

The best way to prevent burnout and interferences from our stated intention of helping others is to commit to self-care on a regular basis. Just as an athlete must do daily stretches and exercises to maintain muscle tone for physical activities, so we need to center ourselves and develop daily programs of energy hygiene. Even when there is nothing amiss and you feel fine, your dedication to learn from the inner laboratory of your daily experiences is essential. Self-reflection is as essential as brushing your teeth.

Journaling is useful in showing you central themes or work areas. An identified meditation place that is just yours in the home is also helpful. Setting a daily time for reflection is mandated in anyone who wishes to help others.

At the beginning of the journey to self-discovery, you may need to be like a detective who notices the slightest shifts in your own energy levels—times you feel depleted, irritated, tense, anxious, or elated. Because most people learn to override subtle emotional signals, more severe symptoms may arise, such as headaches, tiredness, discouragement, intestinal upsets, or frequents colds. When shifts in energy levels are recognized in their early stages, they can easily be corrected with energy balancing methods. Many practitioners find they need to rebalance every few minutes to establish this plane of awareness.

The real gift of inner work, of course, is that whatever we learn about ourselves will also help others. Clients share almost all of the same human dilemmas as we do, such as overcoming procrastination, getting motivated, and staying on task. Clients can go no further in their energy work with their practitioners than the practitioners have, so every step you take to know yourself will be amply rewarded both with personal self-esteem and potential growth for your clients.

Another epithet I have come to respect states, "Either the client gets better or the therapist gets worse." Clients either learn from us and our increasingly balanced energies or their tensions and issues can overwhelm us.

Exercise 5.1 Ongoing Checklist for Self-Reflection

The following questions cover some of the topics we've discussed regarding practitioner care. They can serve to guide the actual practices you develop for personal energy balancing.

1. Do I note when there is rapport between me and my clients? What are the signals?

2. Do I note when rapport with a client is missing? Do I explore what may be happening within myself? Within my client?

3. Can I distinguish between comfortable, positive rapport and the kind of dependencies that may limit me or my clients?

4. Is there anything happening with me that makes it difficult to relate to some clients?

5. Which clients do I most enjoy? With which clients do I have difficulty?

6. Do I tend to project my wishes and attachments onto others?

7. Am I taking care of my personal needs for validation and support? Or do I hope to get this from my clients?

8. Which of my energy centers is most activated with my client's issues?

9. What part of my body feels tense while seeing a specific client or afterward?

10. Do I recognize when I'm working too hard?

11. Do I take time to reevaluate my priorities and redirect my actions? Am I a good CEO of the council of parts within myself?

12. Do I seek more learning within my chosen career? Do I seek learning to increase self-awareness?

Self-reflection along these lines is the foundational resource from which the energy to give generously to others can spring. The wish to help cannot be generated from a mental thought or desire alone. It comes from the seasoned commitment to personal evolution and an unburdened psyche.

There are many more practices to enhance your personal energies than can be listed here. A good place to start, however, is to consider your usual patterns and stretch yourself in new directions.

If you are mostly sedentary, seek physically active energetic practices and classes, such as yoga, tai chi, or qigong, which are well known in Eastern traditions. Western energetic practices include Brain Gym from Educational Kinsesiology,[3] the many "Jump Starts" taught in energy psychology,[4] and the many energy balancing activities taught by Donna Eden.[5] Joining a hiking or environmental organization is valuable because connecting to nature is one of the most nurturing and re-creative energy-enhancing activities.

If you are already quite active physically, you may find deepening practices of mindfulness and meditation helpful. Creative writing is also a fine way to nurture the soul.

Within any lifestyle, seasoned energy health practitioners combine body-oriented and mindfulness practices in some form on a daily basis. It is important to find the path "with heart"—whatever resonates with and most appeals to you—and to make it a regular activity.

Exercise 5.2 Solar Imagery to Nurture the Chakras and Biofield

One of my personal favorite energy meditations, since I live in the far northwest, is to enhance my *qi* with images of the sun. For many people, deprivation of sunlight in autumn and winter is the cause of depression, lethargy, apathy, and other forms of emotional disturbance. Seasonal affective disorder (SAD) is understood as an emotional response in a significant portion of the population. Regular daily exposure to full-spectrum lighting, resembling the emanations of the sun's rays, can alleviate many of the symptoms of SAD. Many people notice emotional changes on rainy or cloudy days. It appears our systems require more *qi* at those times.

Because you have your own imagination and energy system, you may find this exercise helpful in bringing more vitality to your whole body and mind.

1. Stand outside facing the sun and stretch your arms as far back as they will comfortably reach. Feel the warmth of the sun on your arms and bring that warmth into your heart and solar plexus centers with sweeping motions of your arms. Repeat several times with deepening breaths.

2. Especially on cloudy days and indoors, imagine the radiant light of the sun and bring it in from the east or south as in #1 with large, sweeping motions. Breathe in the vibration of sunlight and feel it resonate in your entire body.

3. While either standing in the sun or imagining it, bring this vibration in to your seven major energy centers, starting at the base of the spine. You may want to add an affirmation as you bring your hands over each center and think of its functions.

   • Root chakra: I nurture my aliveness, my right to be fully present in my body.

   • Sacral chakra: I honor my feelings, my ability to choose the people and ideas that fit for me and to release those that do not.

   • Solar plexus: I recognize my ability for clear thinking to make decisions and be effectively assertive.

   • Heart chakra: I radiate caring and goodwill to all around me; I forgive others and myself easily.

   • Throat chakra: I enjoy expressing myself with sounds, words, writing, and other creative means.

   • Brow chakra: I see with insight, intuition, and compassion.

   • Crown chakra: I align my being with the wonder of sunlight, the galaxy, and the universal energy flow.

4. Feel the whole body filling with nourishing sunlight. Let it flow to every cell in your body. Sense sunlight warming each of your internal organs.

5. Sense the fullness of your biofield in all directions and give thanks for being able to appreciate the wondrous presence of the sun and the beauty of the Universe.

* * * *

In dealing with your interferences, shadow material, and distortions in energy flow patterns, you can grow into being the guide toward healing that clients need. Understanding specific vulnerabilities and ways of resolving them is our next consideration for practitioner well-being.

CHAPTER SIX

INCREASING PRACTITIONER INSIGHTS WITH THE CHAKRAS

The chakras are honored in many energy therapies as centers of consciousness and are often used as focal points for treating imbalances in the client's system. In addition, the chakras also serve as a blueprint for enhancing practitioner self-understanding. With the latter in mind, we'll explore relevant aspects from chakra concepts for developing psychological and professional awareness.

The chakras reflect developmental aspects of the human personality, as each energy center is connected to an evolving stage of life and enfolded in the layers of the biofield in hierarchical fashion. Thus, knowledge of vulnerabilities associated with each chakra can assist us as practitioners in understanding how we may unwittingly distort the consciousness of a chakra into self-defeating patterns. Not being aware of these possibilities could lead caregivers to operate outside accepted standards for client care and lead to ethical and even legal dilemmas.

In this chapter, we'll explore the functions of the chakras from a psychological and functional point of view. We'll note practitioner vulnerabilities based on our human desires, wishes, and fears. Possible consequences in practice situations will be considered. We'll also consider possible pathways for resolving conundrums when practitioner needs and professional goals are in conflict.

Overview of the Developmental Energy Centers and Related Practitioner Vulnerabilities

Table 6.1
Overview of the Chakras and Their Psychological Functions

Chakra Name	Location	Physiological Aspects	Physiological Functions
Root or Base	Base of spine	Stress responses, adrenal glands, survival mechanisms	Sense of safety, security, trust—Will to Live
Sacral	Below navel and at sacrum in back	Lower digestive system, reproductive glands	Feelings, sexuality, ability to attract others and release unwanted attentions—Will to Feel
Solar Plexus	Below the sternum (breastbone) and at the back	Upper digestion, pancreas (including cells that produce insulin), liver, and spleen	Clear thinking, self-esteem, healthy self-interest, effective assertiveness—Will to Think
Heart	Mid-chest and corresponding area on back	Heart rhythms, circulation, immune system, thymus gland	Unconditional love, forgiveness, reaching out to others, altruism—Will to Care/Love
Throat	Front and back of neck	Breath, vocal chords, speech, hearing, thyroid glands	Self-expression, creativity, speaking one's truth—Will to Express
Brow	Mid-forehead and back of head	Lower brain functions, sight, taste, smell	Compassion, insight, imagination, intuition, inspiration—Will to See with Insight
Crown	Top of head	Upper brain functions, symbol-making, cognitive processes, connecting to one's biorhythms	Aligning with spirit, connection with one's true nature and purpose—Will to Be

There are many publications that discuss the human energy vortices known as chakras and in varying ways. Table 6.1 is a compilation of the dominant themes and major dynamic elements.[1] The sequence from the base of the spine to the crown holds a progressive pattern that mirrors psychospiritual development in evolving human consciousness. Each stage builds on the previous one so that full human potentials can flourish. When considered as a developmental stage of life, each center has its own issues, choices, values, and behaviors.

Within the chakras lie specific gifts as we move from the most basic needs for safety and survival to increasingly higher consciousness. Within each of the energy centers is the possibility for personal shortfalls if one looks through the filter of human expectations, fears, and sensitivities. Regaining a healthy relationship with self can be accomplished by using the age-old wisdom of the chakras as a blueprint.

To begin, we'll explore each of the centers in light of the needs shared by all human beings and discern possible areas for caregiver misperceptions.

The Root Chakra

Since the root chakra is associated with survival and self-preservation, one obvious area for caregiver infringement is related to finances, the stuff needed to meet the human desire for a guaranteed, steady income to provide food and shelter. Some clients may not wish to invest in the improved health and well-being offered by energy therapies, yet practitioners understandably need money to survive. Thus, practitioner safety and survival may unwittingly be linked to establishing a large practice with many returning clients rather than helping clients to move toward self-reliance. Keeping clients who would actually benefit from other modalities or another practitioner's methods would be an additional infraction in the standard of care mandating that practitioners provide the best possible assistance toward client independence.

The Sacral Chakra

The second chakra is the center of emotional needs and self-gratification. Longings for touch, appreciation, and sexual satisfaction are deep in the human psyche. Clients may misinterpret the helper's comforting touch to fulfill this need and therefore project unrealistic attachments, even romantic ideations, onto the facilitator. Practitioners may themselves long for the deep intimacy that develops in the relationship. Clear boundaries in the areas of touch, comforting, and emotional expression are essential in creating an environment of safety and navigating the tricky waters of human feelings. Transference of client emotions onto the caregiver can create attachment and dependency rather than facilitating increased self-awareness and improved functioning.

The Solar Plexus

The solar plexus is associated with self-definition, personal power, and one's identity in the world. Thus, desires for acceptance, belonging, and status are major issues for caregivers. A possible misuse of power from practitioners is giving advice or attempting to control clients. All practitioners are subject to the power differential because clients will perceive even the most humble caregiver as an empowered being. Another misuse of power would be to use one's special skill and place as caregiver to influence client decision-making. However, being too subdued or unwilling to assist clients in thinking things through also constitutes a misuse of practitioner power.[2] Correct use of power and ego strengths is therefore a major challenge for empowered practitioners.

The Heart Chakra

The heart chakra holds caring energy both vibrationally and psychologically. In addition, the electromagnetic pulses of the heart muscle stimulate brain and body cellular structures to work in harmony with human intention and thought.[3] The caregiver's open heart center allows her to accept clients in their nonactualized states and motivates empathic responsiveness. It is the heart chakra that holds the human desire for unconditional love and acceptance. Distortions of this energy can result in fears of intimacy or professional jealousies. Wanting to be important and seeking approval may cause caregivers to breach confidentiality. More important, too much giving from the heart without concomitant wisdom can cause many helpers to overextend themselves and fall into codependency.

The Throat Chakra

The throat charka is associated with creative self-expression, personal fulfillment, and speaking truth. Helper misperceptions of this energy can result in excessive self-absorption or holding back one's insights. Those patterns can also manifest as frequent criticism of self and others. Another limiting pattern is unwillingness to take responsibility for one's beliefs and actions. Speaking and acting with integrity is essential for practitioners in all therapeutic settings.

The Brow Chakra

The brow center is symbolic of the "third eye" in ancient traditions and is the center of intuition, insight, and compassion. The capacity for compassion engendered by optimal flow of energy in this center allows practitioners to see beyond personal patterns in themselves and their clients. On the other hand, misuse of intuitive powers is a well-known caregiver trap. Some practitioners may inappropriately share their exact perceptions, which can cause clients to feel invaded or confused. Additionally, intuitive hunches can lead to judgments or prejudices that interfere with the values of tolerance and heart-centered caring.

The Crown Chakra

The crown chakra is also affected by human misunderstandings. Loss of the spiritual compass in modern lifestyles is a major concern for many people. Energetic modalities frequently counteract the sense of disconnection from one's Source or Ground of Being. Often, both clients and practitioners will touch into the transpersonal, or more than personal, domains. Vulnerabilities here are that caregivers may use their perceptions to influence clients' spirituality, proselytizing, as it were, for their perceptions of the divine rather than allowing clients to come to their own conclusions and choices. An individual's spiritual path is a unique journey for each person, and the practitioner's role is to carefully support rather than lead or direct clients in their insights. In truth, allowing clients to connect to their own souls is one of the finest gifts the energy modalities offer.

Possible Violations of Professional Standards in Energy Therapy Practices

Since each chakra has vulnerabilities that may cause practitioners to fall short of their highest professionalism, we'll consider each chakra in turn, beginning again at the base of the spine and moving upward toward the more subtle energies of the higher centers. Issues related to the lower three chakras—practitioner survival, the emotions, and personal ego identities—are most associated not only with possible violations of publicly recognized ethics and standards of care, but also with potential legal liabilities.[4]

1. Root Chakra Liabilities

Potential distortions center largely around acting out of insecurity in financially inappropriate ways and/or misrepresenting oneself to augment one's practice income. Specific examples frequently seen among energy healing practitioners are:

- Practicing below publicly accepted standards of care by using a modality that is harmful or not safe for a specific client; not knowing the principles of matching client needs to a specific method or approach; using a "one size-fits-all" method without accounting for individual needs and differences.

- Putting out misleading advertising to bolster one's practice; misrepresenting one's educational or skill level.

- Charging exorbitantly or having improper billing practices; fee-splitting when making referrals.

- Reluctance to refer clients to a more competent practitioner; reluctance to seek supervision or consultation when complex issues arise.

- Being unaware of one's scope of practice, such as making claims beyond one's abilities or education; practicing a profession that is licensed without having the license, for example, doing psychotherapy or in-depth counseling without graduate level education in mental health and being licensed in that discipline.

- Increasing personal income by selling vitamins, devices, or supplements without having the licensed right to prescribe.

Potential legal liabilities that follow from one or more of these behaviors are:[5]

- Criminal prosecution for practicing a licensed profession without a license.

- Criminal prosecution for fraud and misrepresentation.

- Professional discipline for violation of licensing statues and regulations.

- Malpractice and negligence claims for failure to obtain informed consent from a client.

- Prosecution for practicing below standards of care or outside one's scope of practice.

2. Sacral Chakra Liabilities

This chakra is most associated with practitioner feelings and emotional desires. Transgressions may cause a practitioner to act on his feelings without careful thought and assume that clients will understand. Here are the most frequently noted issues:

- Engaging in dual relationships, such as applying treatments casually for friends or at a party; asking for financial advice from a client who is also a stockbroker; letting one's emotions or needs direct decision-making.

- Giving sexual innuendos or engaging in sexual misconduct—examples: making suggestive statements or gestures, using inappropriate language or jokes, hugging in a sexual manner, touching without express client permission.

Potential legal liabilities for misdemeanors in the feeling and sexuality area have received the most publicity because even minor claims of inappropriate sexual gestures or jokes are taken very seriously. Consequences are:

- Criminal prosecution for assault and battery.

- Criminal prosecution for sexual harassment.

- Professional discipline for violating regulations regarding unwanted touch.

- Malpractice or negligence claims for practicing below the standard of care.

3. Solar Plexus Chakra Liabilities

This chakra is related to the caregiver's sense of power and identity. Misunderstanding the reality of the power differential between client and caregiver can result in increased client dependency or sense of being controlled. Frequently noted examples include:

- Making misleading claims of curative ability by exaggerating one's ability to assist with severe conditions.

- Exploiting the power differential by telling a client what to do, imposing one's values, or making decisions for clients.

- Ego-inflation resulting in misrepresenting educational level and skills, such as calling oneself an energy therapist after attending a conference or a weekend workshop only or failing to seek consultation or supervision.

- Failure to obtain informed consent by not fully discussing the treatment plan with clients as partners; failure to explain theory and research base of a method; failure to explain risks and benefits of a modality; ignoring the client's right to choose.

- Ignoring contraindications or precautions by selecting an approach that is inappropriate for a specific client.

Potential legal liabilities are once again many. At the level of the solar plexus, we are reminded that personal pride in caregivers, whether they are licensed or unlicensed, is very costly. The most frequently evoked legal consequences are:

- Criminal prosecution for fraud and misrepresentation.

- Malpractice and negligence claims for failure to obtain client consent.

- Criminal prosecution for assault and battery.

- Professional discipline for violation of licensing statues and regulations.

4. Heart Chakra Liabilities

This energy center is associated with the facilitator's need to be valued and accepted. Distortions of this center can show up in the form of professional jealousies or the need for excessive recognition and praise. Examples include:

- Violating confidentiality by name-dropping a famous client or speaking or writing about clients without adequately disguising or obtaining written consent.

- Seeking friendships through one's professional work by relating to clients in an overly friendly manner; spending time with clients outside the agreed professional parameters.

Potential legal liabilities address breaches of confidentiality quite directly:

- Civil liability for invasion of privacy, breach of confidentiality, and breaches of the trust inherent in the caregiver-client relationship.

- Professional discipline for malpractice and violation of regulations regarding privacy and confidentiality, including HIPAA.

5. Throat Chakra Liabilities

The energy of this center relates to caregiver creativity and self-expression. Taking full responsibility for one's speech and actions requires ongoing willingness to learn and grow. Practitioner shortfalls in this area include:

- Unwillingness to seek consultation for complex issues beyond one's skill level and hoping things will get better without being proactive.

- Unwillingness to speak with integrity in order to confront a client's self-destructive patterns.

Potential legal liabilities are less stringent than with lower chakra issues but include:

- Malpractice and negligence claims.

- Claims of practicing below the accepted standard of care or being outside one's scope of practice.

6. Brow Chakra Liabilities

This chakra is associated with practitioner insights, intuition, and compassion. Misuse of these gifts can severely limit the relationship with clients and lead to prejudices and criticisms. Examples include:

- Bigotry or judgmental attitudes resulting in refusal to work with clients because of race, sexual orientation, or cultural background.

- Misuse of intuited material by implying secret knowledge about a client; interpreting client behavior; "reading energy" of someone without their consent; assuming one's hunches or guesses must be correct.

Potential legal liabilities include:

- Violation of state and federal civil rights statues.

- Malpractice and negligence claims.

- Violation of licensing statutes and professional discipline for practicing below the standards of care.

7. Crown Chakra Liabilities

The energy of this chakra relates to the caregiver's beliefs in a higher power or other forms of transpersonal awareness. Examples of misuse of the power to influence beliefs in others are:

- Addressing spirituality without client consent; "preaching" or telling clients what to believe.

- Failing to address client's surfacing spiritual needs by being either unable to relate to spiritual issues or unwilling to increase one's understanding of spiritual phenomena and nonordinary states of consciousness.

Potential legal liabilities can be found in this deeply personal and subtle domain as well. These may include:

- Prosecution for malpractice and negligence.

- Professional discipline for practicing below the standards of care or for practice outside the scope of practice.

As can be seen from the previous, understanding our vulnerabilities as practitioners can be very helpful in avoiding communication gaps with clients and for preventing legal liabilities. The arenas for overstepping boundaries, cultural parameters, and accumulated wisdom are many in the domains of the lower three chakras—issues related to our safety, survival, feelings, touch, sexuality, and ego identities.

In the higher developmental centers, we encounter challenges more specifically related to energy healing modalities. These include providing heart-centered caring without attachment to outcomes or approval, discussing truth compassionately, appropriately using intuited material, and addressing spiritual needs and issues when requested.

Pathways to Addressing Practitioner Vulnerabilities

The concerns, vulnerabilities, and actual liabilities cited here lead us now to revisit the chakras with strategies for prevention of the most likely pitfalls in our innovative practice of an energy modality. Resolution of internal conflicts is primary when we recognize the reality of human dilemmas that may develop in many arenas. No one can expect the practitioner of energy therapies to be a perfect human being, but it is essential that we make ourselves aware of internal conflicts early on so that we may seek feedback from clients and skilled colleagues. The key here is openness and willingness to learn from every situation.

Take the first chakra vulnerabilities, for example. How could financial pressures on you as a practitioner be lessened? Many healers in other cultures never charge money at all because implied neediness dilutes the healing practitioner's role and distracts from being fully client-centered. My suggestion is either (1) to look at other sources of income rather than making energy therapy practice one's primary source of financial support, or (2) to make sure there are adequate savings and financial planning to avert fiscal dependency on a hand-to-mouth lifestyle. Another important step is to ensure that every piece of marketing material about you, including your website and business card, is accurate and in sync with legal requirements in your community, county, region, and state.

Second chakra issues require taking really good care of your personal needs for touch and intimacy so that those vulnerabilities don't inadvertently slip into client relationships. If you have a primary relationship partner, be sure to maintain the confidentiality of anything you share about clients when you vent emotionally and make sure the partner understands the rules of confidentiality. Do everything possible to have your intimate partner and close friends be the supports you desire and need. If you do not have a partner, awareness of your potential vulnerabilities for emotional neediness should lead you to seek numerous positive supportive settings. These might include regular massage and bodywork, professional workshops away from your community where you can learn more about resources for yourself and your emotional needs, and collegial support groups.

Third chakra awareness requires drawing a fine line between being helpful and coming across as being controlling or pushy in any way. It's just as easy to overpower clients by coming on too strongly as it is to underpower by being too passive. I suggest asking clients to tell you how they feel about any suggestion you make. Better yet, ask clients to make up their own lists of possible choices and help them develop strategies for deciding which one might work best.

Heart-centered issues may cause confusion because all of us want to be liked and appreciated. But it is unlikely that any of us have the intention or personal capability to help relieve human suffering on a 24/7 basis! Therefore, you must understand what a realistic schedule looks and feels like to you, so that you don't overextend yourself. Additionally, if you require unconditional love from others, as most of us do, then make sure you get plenty of this from your partner and close friends rather than seeking it from clients. Furry four-leggeds are unconditionally accepting, so if you live alone, consider getting a pet. Also, be sure to accept and forgive yourself for mistakes while at the same time learning to prevent repeats.

The imperative of the throat chakra leads us to be creative and self-expressive in every endeavor. This would include willingness to learn and implement new skills, to seek activities that give joy, and to be exactingly honest with yourself. Be exquisitely aware of any time you feel uneasy or unsure about an insight. Distinguish what may be helpful to a client from your own needs and issues.

Caution in the area of sharing intuited material with clients is essential so clients don't feel invaded or criticized. In the next chapter, we'll consider more specific ways to enhance intuitive knowing without possible infringements.

Crown chakra issues bring up a wide range of challenges. As facilitators of client energy health, we must be able to work flexibly with total agnostics as well as with those who are spiritual seekers and, of course, with those who hold strong religious beliefs. For many people, connecting to their own energy in the healing environment may be a first encounter with their deeper selves and higher resources. We'll discuss related themes in the next chapter.

Self-affirmations can be very helpful to practitioners who seek to avoid the potential pitfalls along the journey of self-growth. Table 6.2 pairs the many vulnerabilities discussed in this chapter with resolution strategies and related self-affirmations.

Table 6.2
Resources for Addressing Chakra Vulnerabilities

Chakra Name	Examples of Challenges	Sample Resolution Strategies	Sample Affirmations
Root	Financial issues, misrepresentation of skills for competitive advantage	Financial planning, savings, backup career; checking all publicity materials with legal counsel	"I effectively plan for my physical needs; I have always had enough love and money and I always will."
Sacral	Emotional neediness; seeking intimacy	Developing and maintaining intimate relationships outside one's practice; regular bodywork and touch	"I attract the people I need to support me. I am loveable and capable."
Solar Plexus	Misuse of power, overpowering or underpowering	Asking for direct feedback; seeking consultation	"I celebrate my gifts and talents. I actively seek feedback from others."
Heart	Becoming overextended; seeking approval	Listening to personal wishes; scheduling carefully; regular meetings with loved ones	"I ask for what I need and support from those who love me. I accept myself and forgive readily."
Throat	Limiting creativity & self-expression; holding back	Learning new skills; engaging in fun activities, speaking to clients with integrity	"I enjoy my creativity; I explore new gifts and talents. I speak my truth with compassion."
Brow	Appropriate use of intuition	Finding appropriate ways to use intuited material	"I honor my perceptions and share them in ways that can best be received by my clients."
Crown	Spiritual needs; personal beliefs	Sensitivity in relating to people without specific spiritual values as well as with firm believers	"I value my faith, my personal spiritual path. I honor the different beliefs of others."

The resolution strategies and affirmations suggested here help to build a resource I like to call the "inner advisor." Close attention to the foundational work of developing one's inner therapist allows us, as practitioners, to be sensitive to our own areas of uneasiness and thereby diminish risks. Likewise, the golden standard of seeking competent consultation is an essential part of any professional practice, especially in the new and relatively uncharted territories of energy therapies.

CHAPTER SEVEN

EXTENDING PRACTITIONER ENERGIES TO INCLUDE INTUITITIVE AND TRANSPERSONAL DOMAINS

Connecting to Intuition

As energy therapy practitioners develop their skills in sensing client energy fields, intuition or hunches about client situations quite naturally emerge. The framework we've established of a right, healing relationship with oneself and personal centering lends objectivity to these insights. Overdependence on one's intuition as a primary guide in energy therapy practice, however, can lead to several traps:

- Clients may feel disempowered when the helper appears to know more about them than they do.

- Clients may find intuition quite odd or foreign to their way of thinking.

- The practitioner's hunch may be more of a personal projection rather than material that is actually relevant to the client.

- Even if a practitioner's speculation is correct in the sense that it fits with client history, the client may not be ready to receive it; when such "hits" are shared without the client's consent, the rapport of the relationship is impaired.

The following questions thus need to be addressed in regard to the appropriate use of intuition:

- How do I strengthen my higher sense perceptions?

- How do I know what I sense or guess is the client's material and not my own projection?

- What is the best way to handle images or strong messages I get about a client?

- How can I empower my clients with the use of these perceptions?

Respect for the client's needs must be the core value in handling intuited material. Slipping into third chakra power distortions with such material could violate the standard for sensitivity to the power differential. Furthermore, accepting an intuition as truth blinds the practitioner to considering the many factors involved in client dilemmas.

One common source of sixth chakra distortion is projection of one's personal issues onto the client. For example, practitioners who have authority problems may unwittingly assume that all clients have issues with authority. Alternately, therapists who dislike their own neediness may sense dependency issues in all of their clients. Practitioners who have themselves been victims of abuse may see clients as victims of their dilemmas and therefore be overly sympathetic and lack objectivity. Thus, knowing your own issues through self-insight will make you less likely to assume that the same issues belong to your clients.

Fanciful interpretations of client issues when practitioners assess or work in another person's energy field may actually be a form of spiritual voyeurism. Utmost care must be exercised to avoid bringing judgment, possible criticisms, or misleading information to clients during and after energy treatments. When clients ask for practitioner perceptions about an area of energetic blockage, it's best to deflect the query and ask the client, "What might this mean to you?" Alternately, you could offer, "Let's explore together the meaning and ways to relieve this disturbance."

Another example of misguided intuition arises when a practitioner experiences bodily sensations while helping a client and interprets these feelings as signifying unknown client symptoms. In the past, some healers used personal somatic sensations to guess at client needs, but such methods are quite dangerous because they stress the caregiver's body. Such an approach is also subject to projections. The real goal of a helpful therapy is to teach clients to learn from their own bodily symptoms, to explore their emotional and physical pain, and to find motivation for change.

Asking questions about something the practitioner suspects is much less invasive and off-putting. For example, "Was there abuse in your childhood?" is much less confrontational than saying, "I get a strong hit that you were abused as a child, maybe sexually or physically, or both. Oh, and I get that your father was the abuser." By asking a question, the client has the choice to consider the issue, to pass if he's not ready to deal with it, or to think about it for future reference.

Since many energy therapy practitioners use aids to intuition, such as a pendulum, medicine cards, or muscle testing, a word is in order about their use. Despite obvious enthusiasm for these aids, they are not absolutely reliable or infallible. Depending on many factors, including the intentions of both practitioner and client, answers can easily be obfuscated. These tools may assist in giving input to decision-making but should never be used to the exclusion of other approaches, such as common sense, objective evaluation, consultation, and attention to developing one's inner knowing. It is simply not a good idea to make major life choices based on testing relative muscle strength or the use of a pendulum!

Accessing Inner Wisdom

Practitioners' inner wisdom can be enhanced with practice and through conscious choice. As you learn to develop this connection, you can use it to enhance your personal vitality and sense of direction. It can also serve as an effective ally in your relationship with clients as you seek insights from less well-known parts of yourself.

Here is a suggestion for developing this higher sense perception and connecting to your own inner therapist.

Exercise 7.1 Establishing Internal Dialogue

1. After centering, allow your mind to wander to relevant questions, such as: What is my best course of action for the future (name a situation coming up)? How can I best help my next client (include the name)? Write down the question you want to focus on.

2. Take several deep breaths and allow your consciousness to lift through the chakras, the field, and beyond the body. See yourself without judgment or criticism. Sense kindness flowing from the vast resources of nature to your unique being.

3. Restate your question mentally and write down any thoughts that come to you.

4. Anytime the flow stops, ask, "Is there anything else?" Trust that there is a higher, wiser aspect of yourself that comes with each next breath.

5. Notice any particular voice or image (a person, an animal, an angel, a guide) that is associated with what you receive. This may or may not happen for you and is certainly not required. Just enjoy what comes to you from the deeper, more sensitive aspects of yourself.

6. When you sense that you are complete, extend thankfulness to all parts of yourself and to any perceived helpers. Appreciate how there is always more to learn from your inner being, your very best friend.

7. Gently, come back to full awareness, feeling your breath, and read without judgment what came to you. Do this exercise often until it becomes a natural part of your preparation for the day, for new clients, or a pending decision.

Accessing the Transpersonal Domain

Evolution to spiritual perceptions appears to be a natural part of most energy practitioners' development. Connecting to inner wisdom also expands our appreciation for the divine spark that lies within. For many, there is a sense of a higher consciousness that seems to guide and influence our life's journey. This path appears to unfold from higher sources, beyond our ego selves—it is transpersonal, or beyond the purely personal.

We live in a world of energy. Our sun, with its vast, ongoing dynamic of fusion from hydrogen to helium, radiates the warmth and light that make life possible on Earth. Even this vibrant solar energy is but a small sampling of the seemingly unlimited energies that coalesced to form the "big bang" that started the universe in is present direction more than thirteen billion years ago. Whether we believe in a personal God or not, thinking people must be filled with a sense of awe and wonder at contemplating the reality of the tremendous *qi* that is present in our universe.

The sense of deep awe and respect for the creative force that resides in each person guides us as practitioners. Each person, no matter how distraught, is one aspect of Big Mind, embodied in human form, an opening for the Absolute to manifest. Part of our development as practitioners is to grow in understanding our life's purpose and to stretch beyond our personalities to the limitless energies in the universe.

In energy therapies, there is a felt sense that all of us are interconnected beyond our temporary human manifestations. Many practitioners have had the experience of feeling deeply linked with others who live far away or with loved ones who are no longer alive. The energetic bonds appear to be timeless, beyond limited, localized understandings. Even personal physical death can be viewed as a transition—a prelude to a wider dream that can be as imaginative as one wishes it to be.

The transpersonal is not defined by social or religious affiliations. Instead, it reflects each individual's quest for spiritual understanding, for finding one's place and sense of meaning within the vast sea of galaxies. Defining ourselves as spiritual beings within the current world so filled with uncertainties can decidedly bring a sense of hope and inner peace.

Connecting to the ground of our being opens doors to trusting not only our intuition but also to sensing higher guidance. It allows each person, both practitioner and client, to be filled with the opportunity for unlimited potential. It widens curiosity about the future and permits the facing of perils with confidence and faith. It helps inform our path even when we are not sure about our best next steps.

Ultimately, our clients seek ways of accessing their own inner knowing and the inner confidence of trust in something greater than themselves. The more we learn to give language and meaning to our own path, the more readily we can assist our clients. The more we as practitioners can light the way to help clients experience alignment with the Infinite, the more they can feel grounded and nurtured. At times, clients' paths may lead them to nonordinary states of consciousness, unusual ways of meeting their inner wisdom. We'll explore some of these possibilities and how practitioners can assist clients to find maps through uncharted territories of their own subconscious material in a subsequent chapter.

Transpersonal Aspects of Healing

All healing endeavors are essentially a form of spiritual questing. Some clients will verbalize a sense of connecting to a higher power during or after an energy intervention. Others will simply hold the feeling of reconnecting to themselves at a deeper level. In either case, it seems clear that giving an energy therapy method is, in essence, participation in the client's transpersonal healing journey. This awareness helps us to honor the sacredness of the relationship. Have you noticed how often the specific needs of the client actually match the very gifts you have to share? It is as if individuals with specific issues are drawn to us as practitioners when we have the very resources they most need.

Although the mechanics of an energetic interaction may look deceptively simple—therapist's hands assess the field, modulate energy, hold the chakra energies, or stimulate meridian acupoints—the inner process between practitioner and client is exceedingly complex when we consider the many dimensions that are touched, often with minimal or no actual physical touching. Dr. Dolores Krieger, founder and leader of Therapeutic Touch (TT), the first and most-recognized energy modality to enter mainstream healthcare, writes, "Most often it is only through mature practice that one realizes that TT is an absorbing dynamic of unsounded depth. Moreover, both the TT therapist and the healee engaged in this multidimensional process are unequivocally open systems of vibrant, human energies, each set clothed in its own intentionalities, enactments, and visions."[1] She continues to develop and expand her concept of energy treatments as an opening to the sacred, a way of honoring the very sanctity of life. The inner development of the practitioner is birthed in compassion and matures into conscious communication with the inner self.

The mindful, centered focus of the caregiver connects with the client to facilitate communication with wider levels of self, including transpersonal realms, nonordinary states of consciousness, and in other forms. All levels of consciousness are involved in the healing process. In a non-deistic style, Dr. Krieger elaborates on the transpersonal realm: "At the farther reaches of consciousness appear to be those personal qualities that make up the deep center of one's individuality....The spiritual level of consciousness is the individual's link with the universal base of consciousness itself."[2]

From this perspective, we surmise that a healing practice is a moving meditation between two energy beings held within the safe context of their connection to universal *qi*. The practitioners who allow themselves to be filled with this energy, as they center and align with the *Big Qi*, begin to radiate their own light and generally have improved overall health. As we align with our sense of purpose and guiding direction, our personal satisfaction increases. As we allow ourselves to be inspired, we have the energy and resources to assist many others—without fatigue.

The ethic of caring from this transpersonal perspective is not so much about action, or *doing*, but rather about who we are, our *being*. Words about the transpersonal may never be spoken, but the reality of it exists in a felt sense. Discussions about the transpersonal domain succeed best if clients themselves initiate them and they are then explored in a way that is comfortable and noninvasive.

* * * *

In this chapter, we've considered the domains of intuition and the transpersonal, which are integral in the practices of many energy-oriented caregivers. I've inserted notes of caution with the intention of helping you to achieve the professional standard of "walking your talk," doing inner work to know and understand the many realms you may touch in clients. Coming from inner wisdom to be fully present to clients is a lifelong, and wonderfully rewarding, journey for all practitioners.

Vignettes for Section II

Vignette II.1 Behind Schedule All Too Often!

Gina was an effective energy practitioner, so much so that her calendar was always full. She liked giving extra time to those with special needs. Ten minutes here, a little more time there, and by the end of the day she was several hours off. Clients grumbled, the waiting room energy was palpably heavy, and Gina was exhausted every evening.

After her medical doctor found high blood pressure and early symptoms of diabetes, Gina recognized that she needed help in organizing better. She found a reliable therapist for herself and learned to apply principles of stress management. It took over a year of personal work, clocks, timers, affirmations, and meditations for Gina to establish control over her timing. With these daily actions, she learned to honor the ethic of true caring by starting with herself—at home.

Vignette II.2 Missing the Most Important Part

Terry was an established counselor who felt confident in understanding client needs. Bob was referred to Terry by a colleague who knew Terry's energy therapy could help release trauma. In the waiting room, Bob filled out the forms given and added a long list of symptoms as well as the lawsuits he had going against several past practitioners.

Terry did not read the document, assuming the client came in good faith. He was focused on showing his colleague how effective the energy methods could be. Bob seemed lukewarm to the energy methods Terry taught him, but Terry did not note Bob's lack of rapport or discuss feelings about the treatment he received.

A month later, Terry received a filed complaint from his Board of Behavioral Sciences citing that Terry had not honored Bob's rights, had not respected Bob's listing of problems, and had instituted a series of procedures that were strange and undocumented. Bob was obviously a litigious client.

Since only one session was held and Bob did admit he felt better afterward, the board ruled that the matter could be settled out of court, provided both parties could come to a settlement. After many months of paperwork, inner turmoil, and consultation with legal and professional counsels, Terry settled the case by paying a large sum and was placed on probation by the board for a year. Because of haste and overconfidence, Terry lost more than he could gain. The whole situation on an "off day" was a difficult lesson in humility.

Discussion: If Terry had taken the time to get full information from Bob, he might have been able to establish a relationship that could deal with Bob's mistrust. Instead, Terry relied on his experience and assumptions rather than seeing the client as he really presented. Overconfidence blinded him to the issues where humility and asking for feedback could have saved an enormous amount of time and money. Also, Bob lost out on the opportunity to gain an understanding practitioner; the delicate thread that establishes healthy relationships was permanently broken in this case.

Vignette II.3 Holding Center in the Face of Adversity

Kim, a nurse practitioner in a small integrative healthcare center, was authorized to use energy modalities within the scope of practice of her nursing license. However, one of the other practitioners at the center felt that use of such innovative methods was not appropriate and filed a complaint with the relevant state agency. Although there was no fault on Kim's part, it took her six painful months of letters and appeals to clear herself.

During this time, Kim was anxious and her body actually shook whenever she saw the accusing colleague. One day she decided she had had enough—she had done no wrong. The colleague was not willing to understand the new paradigm of energy work. Kim started actively centering herself even when just thinking about her office and almost continuously when she entered the building. She used chants and loving-kindness meditations to stay in a nonviolent, nonharming position toward the colleague.

After the final dismissal of the claims came, the complainant left the integrative practice, rather ashamed of herself. With the help of strong and effective self-care, Kim weathered the storm.

Vignette II.4 All Boxed In!

Lisa had been an effective energy health practitioner for several years when she received referral of a prominent businessman named Jack. He had a seemingly hopeless immune disorder. Lisa checked and documented that all conventional medical procedures had been done before he was referred for complementary therapies.

Lisa saw Jack twice a week for three weeks to establish strong transference and help to balance his energies. Jack showed marked improvement of symptoms and both were delighted with the outcome. Treatment continued once a week after the initial "push."

As Jack improved, Lisa began to notice him in a more personal way: a lonely, single man who was exceedingly grateful for the help he was receiving. Lisa looked forward to seeing him regularly and began to notice the growing attraction between them.

Lisa was hesitant to change the pattern of treatment they had set up since it was working so well. She became fearful that referral to another therapist would make him lose much of the valuable ground he had gained. Also, she had made several financial commitments based on the steady income of the weekly sessions. Lisa was afraid to see a colleague for consultation about the uneasiness the attraction caused her because she was afraid the colleague could hurt her reputation.

All boxed in when the ability to treat was in conflict with her feelings and she was seemingly unable to get help—what should she do?

Discussion: Several chakra issues are apparent here: financial need (first chakra), possible romantic involvement (second chakra), attachment to outcomes and the ego needs of being the unique caregiver (third chakra), and fear of exposure with possible loss of reputation and approval to another person (first and fourth chakras).

To resolve such a multilevel dilemma, consultation is essential. Consultation, of course, is always confidential. It is the hallmark of ethical practice to seek consultation from one or more competent professionals who are not personal friends. The power differential between caregiver and client demands that the practitioner be fully alert to her needs and possible transference or codependency issues.

Ideally, Lisa should select a recognized competent practitioner or consultant to assist her in sorting out feelings and setting priorities. In all likelihood, just discussing her feelings would help Lisa to recognize the conflict and chose to set care of the client as a priority. If Lisa were truly unable to do this, she should refer the client to another competent practitioner.

Most states require a two-year waiting period between termination of therapy with a licensed mental health professional and the onset of a dating relationship. Other states hold that client relationships should never evolve into personal romance. Although these tenets may be difficult to enforce, the intention of the regulation is to protect clients from the subtle invasion of personal space that is inherent in the therapeutic relationship and to function within clear, established boundaries from the outset.

Vignette II.5 Overcoming Practitioner Resistance

Meg studied energy therapies for several years and was able to achieve excellent results with clients who had long-term posttraumatic stress disorder (PTSD) due to childhood trauma. Nancy was a new client who showed marked symptoms of PTSD with anxiety, agoraphobia, nightmares, and withdrawal from life.

Meg intuitively sensed that there was childhood molestation and that she could help Nancy release the symptoms by attuning to the client's early childhood memories. Unfortunately, Nancy could not recall any such event and did not want to address the issue in the way that Meg recommended. Meg felt her ability to help Nancy was blocked by this "resistance." What should she do?

Discussion: Actually, the burden for "resistance" in this case lies with the therapist for having such set ideas about how treatment should proceed. It's important to understand that clients may have hundreds of conscious and unconscious reasons for not being able to recall childhood events. The work of a skilled facilitator is to respect the client's inner process and trust that memories will surface when the psyche feels safe and protected.

In the meantime, Meg has numerous options for working energetically with this client. She could teach energy balancing methods for client self-care. She could work to enhance rapport and trust. She should definately look at her own judgments about client resistance.

Since it is estimated that nearly 60 percent of first-time clients never return for a second session, practitioners are often left with the frustration of not knowing what the client is thinking and feeling. The first session may be the only opportunity to create a safe space in which clients feel heard and understood. It is a fine art to know how to attend to stated wishes from the client and offer at least one approach for relief in the very first meeting. It is incumbent on practitioners to release their attachments to specific outcomes and to be fully present to client needs, without emotional baggage.

Vignette II.6 "Where Is God When I Need Him/Her?"

Susan was drawn to energy therapies because of her strong intuitive nature and spiritual questing. She understood *qi* flow patterns and wanted to learn how to help her husband, who was in the late stages of dying from cancer. Rita, her energy practitioner, noted frequently recurring blocked energies in Susan's system because of the stress she was carrying as primary caregiver for the husband. Both agreed the treatment plan would be to help Susan maintain health and vitality through this difficult time.

Susan despaired because she could not seem to help her husband at all. After several nights of no sleep due to his pain, she cried, out, "Where is God when I need him or her or whoever?"

Because the question was framed spiritually, Rita encouraged Susan to continue exploring her understanding of who and what God might be in face of the pressing realities. Rita also made sure Susan received medical treatment for her insomnia and helped to arrange for a home health aide to spend several nights with the patient until Susan could reestablish a regular sleep pattern.

Susan began to think God was more than "just a nice guy." Perhaps, they both considered together, God is the ineffable energy that supports us in difficult times and when we don't have easy answers. Perhaps, the grace of energy therapy is even more relevant to the person who takes care of a patient than the ill person. The patient has his own inner journey toward the end of life while the caregiver, in this case Susan, had the task of finding a new way to live.

As time went on, and the husband's life energy faded, Susan became more comfortable in accepting the end-of-life changes that were beyond her understanding. Meditation and prayer helped her to relax and face the serious learning adventure life had given her. Rita was the ongoing steady anchor during the time of the husband's passing. Deep transpersonal sharing, often without words, and holding each other's hands enriched the relationship and empowered both of them.

Vignette II.7 What Did I Get Myself Into?

Energy practitioner Patti often liked to do extra things for her clients. When pitiful Carol showed up, her heart overflowed with compassion. Carol had no money, so the sessions were free. Later, it turned out that

Carol had no car, so Patti helped her buy groceries and transported her from place to place. Often, Patti paid for the groceries when she realized that Carol would not have anything to eat. A few weeks later, when Carol lost her home due to a deal gone bad, Patti took Carol into her home.

Over time, Patti realized that Carol's needs were a bottomless pit. Things came to a head when Patti's daughter needed a place to stay and Patti told Carol to find another place to live. Carol was furious at being evicted and eventually went to an attorney to get money from Patti's insurance by claiming that Patti had engaged in malpractice and negligence. What should Patti do?

Discussion: This is an extreme but actual case. It was, unfortunately, a bit late to teach Carol needed life skills and seek community resources for someone so apparently hapless. Patti needed to learn to face her own lack of boundaries and misperceptions about the practitioner role. Early intervention with consultation for any action that might be deemed an overextension would have helped reduce the risky behavior sequence.

The case was settled out of court with a large payment from Patti since the judge ruled that she had been negligent as a practitioner for not using social services to help Carol at the outset. Of course, the person Patti had most truly neglected was herself.

SECTION III:

STANDARDS FOR CREATING HEALING RELATIONSHIPS WITH CLIENTS

Always do the right thing—
it will confound some and satisfy the others.
—Mark Twain, author and humorist

Ethical Principle:

Practitioners of energy therapies consider each client's needs in physical, emotional, mental, and/or spiritual dimensions as their priority when providing care.

Related Standards of Practice:

- Energy therapy practitioners (ETPs) set their intention for the highest good of each client, relinquishing any attachments, personal agendas, or desires for specific outcomes.

- ETPs base their care on theory, knowledge, and research in relation to the human energy system and make sure clients understand their right to informed consent.

- ETPs continually evaluate client outcomes and plans of care, seeking supervision and/or consultation as needed.

- ETPs set clear boundaries with clients regarding permissions, meeting place, time, fees, confidentiality, contact between sessions, etc.

- ETPs communicate clearly with clients about clients' expectations and about the results they may realistically expect, both at the outset and as the healing relationship evolves.

- When a questionable situation arises, ETPs carefully and respectfully inquire about the client's perceptions, motivations, and stakes in the matter. They think things through, gather pertinent information, and seek consultation when needed.

- ETPs stay aware of power dynamics, particularly the unequal "power" they have as a practitioner when expressing opinions, offering assessments, or otherwise influencing clients to think or act in certain ways.

- If a situation arises in relation to the client that causes discomfort, concern, or misgivings, ETPs bring the matter to conscious attention and actively work to resolve it—long before it manifests as a problem.

- ETPs recognize when client issues exceed their skill level and refer to appropriate other professional resources.

- ETPs do their utmost to avoid dual or complex relationships.

Chapter Eight

The Fiduciary Relationship in Energy Therapies

A central standard for all healthcare professionals is to comprehend fully the implications of the fiduciary relationship. Derived from the Latin word *fiducia,* this relationship is one of explicit trust and confidence, such as clients place in a professional. The legal term "fiduciary relationship" refers to an affiliation in which one party places trust in an identified professional. The client or patient is, in effect, putting his well-being in the hands of the caregiver. This implies agreement that the practitioner will always place the client's needs and interests above his or her own.

Founded on faith and trust, public confidence in individuals who present themselves as energy healers, lightworkers, or practitioners of one of the many energy therapies depends on the values and actual practice standards upheld by each person. Thus it is imperative that practitioners carefully support the elements that enhance and reinforce client trust. Over time, public credibility and acceptance for our new, innovative methods can grow just as confidence in allied healthcare professions, such as nursing and physical therapy, has developed over the past several decades. Good news of consumer satisfaction with energy therapies is spreading slowly but steadily, despite the fact that there are as yet no specific public requirements or rules for practice. The reasons for satisfaction include practitioner willingness to be fully present to clients, their ability to take time, their compassionate styles, and the reality that many people obtain physical and emotional relief via energetic approaches.[1] Often, the limitations of conventional, Western medicine appear to dissolve when energetic principles are included in treatment of the whole person.

Bad news travels quickly, and any unpleasant client experience can be publicly known even more rapidly via today's communication technology. Clients are not bound to confidentiality, as practitioners are. And it is well known that some practitioners of conventional formats wish to debunk energy therapies by looking for any breaches of fiduciary trust or treatment irregularities.[2] Utmost care must, therefore, be taken to protect and guard the vulnerable bond of positive transference with clients—and to respect the essence of the fiduciary relationship. The power differential implied in clients' trust means practitioners have to hold themselves to a higher standard of self-awareness and behavior than other people.

Here is a summary of the major standards for practice that directly build and support the trust clients place in anyone who serves to alleviate emotional distress. They are therefore highly relevant to all licensed or unlicensed energy therapy practitioners. This list is compiled from the ethical standards required of mental health practitioners by the state licensing boards of the disciplines who are involved in the counseling/mental health field:

Level of Competence

- Practice only in areas in which you have extensive learning and competence.

- Maintain competence and stay current in your training.

- Make accurate representation of your credentials and know your scope of practice.

- Seek skilled consultation whenever uneasy.

- Make appropriate referrals when needed.

- Handle referrals and termination so client does not feel abandoned.

Record Keeping

- Document that informed consent has been given with benefits, risks, and client choice when introducing any new methodology.

- Document that adequate medical evaluation and/or ongoing care is present.

- Keep records of date and description of services for consultation and legal reasons.

- Hold all client records in strictest confidence, even after termination.

Professional Responsibility

- Conform to accepted ethics and standards of practice for counseling disciplines.

- Obtain informed consent throughout treatment planning and implementation.

- Avoid discredit to your profession.

- Decline participation in third-party discussions about other professionals; if a concern arises, deal with the person involved directly.

- Use nonexploitative business practices.

- Report potential or actual danger related to clients or colleagues.

Boundaries

- Do not become sexually involved with any client.

- Take responsibility for setting and maintaining professional boundaries, such as meeting time and place, fees, policy for no shows, telephone or internet communications, recommendations, referrals, etc.

Confidentiality

- Safeguard all information obtained while providing services—including the fact that the person is or was a client.

- Adequately disguise any confidential information used for teaching or research.

- Hold information in confidence even after termination.

- Know the three legally required exceptions to confidentiality.

Marketing

- Ensure that all marketing materials represent your credentials and scope of practice accurately.

- Indicate via disclaimers on your materials, including website, that reading the material does not constitute a professional relationship, medical advice, or other form of agreement.

- Seek legal counsel to make sure all marketing materials meet the accepted standards in the community where you will practice.

In addition to these essential elements that from the foundation of the fiduciary relationship, energy therapy practitioners are called upon to pay attention to the unique qualities that arise in the use of energy therapies. Factors such as rapid rapport, quick release of distress, activation of unconscious material, connection to archetypal patterns, and the presence of nonordinary states of consciousness call for even *greater* care in establishing healing, positive client relationships. For our discussion of these unique elements we'll focus on the following themes:

- Careful attention to the client's informed consent with information that includes theory, science, and research.

- Documentation that informed consent is given and that the client has freely chosen the selected method.

- Full disclosure of benefits and possible risks involved with innovative energy modalities.

- Attention to nuances that may indicate client's reluctance or lack of full agreement.

- Repeated emphasis on client's right to choose or refuse a suggested method.

- Consensual goal setting and treatment planning.

- Ongoing awareness of the power differential between caregiver and client.

- Protecting and maintaining boundaries that have been mutually set, even if the client requests or instructs the helper to do otherwise.

- Unwavering attention to confidentiality and permissions.

The issues of fiduciary relationships become more pronounced in therapeutic contracts that involve energy approaches. The caregiver attunes to client needs not only verbally, but also intuitively and from perceptions of the client's energies. Decisions as to which method to institute are based on information received from the multidimensional client biofield.

Additionally, some clients are intensely aware of practitioner energy levels and may, as a result of these sensitivities, respond to issues that are outside the caregiver's conscious awareness. While an estimated 20 percent of the general population are highly sensitive people,[3] it's fair to assume that people seeking energy therapists are much more likely to have sensitivities and perceptions beyond the more usually known cognitions.

We'll explore the specific nature for safeguarding client relationships as we consider the interaction of human biofields and the many dimensions of the sacred contract in subsequent chapters. Here, let's consider each of the previously cited elements that support establishing healthy relationships with our clients.

Informed Consent

Informed consent means that you as the practitioner give clients a clear idea of each method you will be using as well as the related theory base, known research, and proof of effectiveness and safety. Interestingly, this concept of information disclosure to the client's level of understanding is also a well-understood risk management process, as we learned in the discussion of legalities in chapter 3. Some clients will want to know specific references, books, articles, and website resources. Others may be content with simpler explanations. In either case, being prepared with documentation gleaned from your studies and continuing education is essential. Carefully pacing the explanation and demonstration of your approach to the client's curiosity, questions, and ability to comprehend is therefore important.

Another element of informed consent is for clients to be fully cognizant of known benefits of the modality you will use, as well as to consider the possible risks. The benefits of most energy-oriented methods are many and include release of felt distress, enhanced immune function, decreased anxiety, deep relaxation, increased sense of personal efficacy, improved self-esteem and self-insight, and a sense of personal empowerment.[4] Another major benefit is that many of the methods can be adapted for self-care so clients can use them on their own and as needed.

Risks are less frequently mentioned because many practitioners are eager to champion their chosen modality. While enthusiasm for one's approach is undoubtedly a fine quality, knowing possible risks is essential as well. Especially from a psychological viewpoint, there are substantial interpersonal risks with energy therapies depending on client issues and needs. For example, the change in some clients' moods can happen so rapidly that they end up with cognitive dissonance, actually disbelieving themselves and the real change that has occurred. If a client holds the belief that it takes a long time to release trauma, he may be disappointed, even jarred, by a rapid, heretofore unknown, freedom from fears and a sudden inflow of peacefulness.

Another well-documented risk is that the problem or trauma will feel less pressing: the client may feel some distance from it and therefore will be unable to recall specific aspects of a traumatic event. While this is a desirable outcome from a therapeutic point of view, it is an impediment to anyone who needs to go through legal procedures for making insurance claims, giving a deposition, or being a plaintiff in a court of law.

Furthermore, a change in one's view of the world and self-identity may evolve via rapid mind-body integrations that occur with use of energy methods. While these outcomes could be desirable for the individual, they could seriously affect surrounding social systems, such as a career or family situations that hold rigid boundaries and defined role expectations.

Another often-noted risk is the holographic nature of the work. The client may get relief from a presenting problem only to find another deeper or more central issue that comes to conscious awareness. Again, this is beneficial in the long run, but may be confusing if the client expects immediate and simple solutions.

Energy therapy practitioners take utmost care to make clients aware of the wide range of benefits and risks that may result from their participation in the work. It is best to encourage clients to consider the possibilities of far-reaching changes and to conclude whether such developments are in line with the client's intentions and goals. If the practitioner chooses not to use a written form to demonstrate client understanding of informed consent, documentation that a discussion of the pertinent aspects of this agreement has been given should be in the client file. (A sample form for written consent is given in appendix B.)

Client Right to Choice

Empowering clients to make considered choices for themselves is an optimal outcome of any therapeutic relationship. The reality of each client's right to choose may need to be underscored frequently within each step of an intervention process. The healer must not only be able to ensure written and/or verbal agreement, but must also pay attention to the subtle nuances that may indicate when something is out of sync. Practitioners therefore need to be fully aware of both verbal and nonverbal assent to any given procedure.

Client doubts may show up in hesitation, asking many questions, or being overly enthusiastic. Intuitive sensitivity from the caregiver may be needed to assess facets of the client that are not fully in her awareness. The more practitioners can resort to a large range of approaches to bring about relief, the more successful they can be in helping their clients. A small gain may be what is needed to establish client confidence via other, more traditional methods you have to offer. For example, a client may not be sure about releasing her trauma just yet, but a resourceful practitioner can teach body focusing exercises, diaphragmatic breathing, and the use of imagery to help alleviate anxiety.

Another fine practitioner skill is creativity in matching a specific method to client needs. Flexible practitioners have a deep commitment to ongoing learning to develop a compendium of resources for their clients.

The Power Differential

Despite attempts from facilitators to be as compassionate and client-centered as possible, most clients will still relate to the caregiver as an empowered being or authority figure. Some of this dynamic is present due to basic patterns or archetypes that are often unconscious parts of human interactions, such as Parent/Child, Teacher/Student, Authority/ Subject, Master/Slave. (These patterns and their impact on the healing relationship are discussed in chapter 11.) For this reason, clients will often agree to any practitioner suggestion or intuition because the helper is seen as the empowered professional and person in charge.

Practitioners themselves may unconsciously choose methods they like best and present them in more appealing ways than ideas proposed by clients. They may unwittingly have substantial attachments to using a certain technique, in the form of a hidden personal agenda.

A good way to track the power differential is for the caregiver to engage in self-assessment of each client session. Hindsight is an excellent way to potentiate skills for being in the present moment, the "here and now," of future sessions.

Exercise 8.1 Tracking Right Use of Power in Relation to Clients

A personal, private notebook for evaluating your energy practice sessions is a helpful ally in considering your learning from each session. This notebook is different from clinical notes and regular documentation of each meeting, which is a necessary part of the client record and can, under extreme conditions, be part of a legal defense on your behalf.

Jot down your reflections on each of the following questions:

1. How did I empower the client to make choices for herself?

2. Did I present several methods from which to choose?

3. How did the method chosen help the client?

4. Did I have a personal agenda in suggesting it?

5. What alternative approaches might I use in a subsequent session?

6. How often did I ask the client for her opinion or feedback?

7. Was rapport present in the session?

8. Where there times I became distracted?

9. Did my enthusiasm for energy therapy come from a desire to demonstrate what I know?

10. Was there clear agreement to use the selected method?

11. How did I encourage and give room for a reluctant or passive client to express her feelings and attitudes?

If you notice any personal doubts arising from this evaluation, you might want to plan a meeting with your inner healer, your own guidance, or your mentor/consultant. A vastly helpful standard in any profession is having an established consultative relationship for evaluating your practice and your personal understandings. Professional judgment to discriminate which clients fare best with selected methods develops gradually over time. A more seasoned guide can help you mature into your chosen field and minimize the distortions possible within the power differential.

Mutual Treatment Planning

Respectful, client-centered practice begins with mutual goal-setting. Exploring client expectations is necessary because many people seek energy practices to meet their internal agendas. Patients in pain, for example, have frequently been to numerous physicians and practitioners before turning to energetic approaches. Their expectations for immediate relief with energy approaches can be quite unrealistic. Most practitioners will agree that they cannot predict outcomes, but they can state that, based on previous experience, clients may experience some form of relief and increased relaxation.[5] Thus a realistic goal for a session might be to hold the possibility that there may be pathways to relaxation with decreasing pain of one or several percentage points.

Recognizing small gains over two or three sessions can help both client and practitioner evaluate whether energetic methods will be helpful or whether another modality might be more appropriate. The idea that the practitioner is aware of referral and consultation resources, and is likely to use them if indicated, should be presented at the outset of client-practitioner agreements.

Clients need to bring in their understandings as well. They should agree to speak truth, to give honest feedback, to do no harm, and to express their wishes and needs in each session.

Other elements of the therapeutic contract include mutual agreements about time and place of meeting; frequency of contacts; whether telephone or e-mail communications are desirable and, if so, how frequently; fees or an agreed-on barter exchange that does not distort the fiduciary relationship; time for evaluation of the treatments at the end of each session; and discussions about confidentiality and permissions.

Confidentiality

Keeping confidences is an accepted part of the fiduciary relationship. There are exceptions by law to confidentiality in most states under certain circumstances: (1) if abuse of a minor child or dependent elderly person is revealed, it must be reported to the appropriate state agency; (2) if the client indicates active suicidal ideation with a plan, a significant family member must be informed; (3) if a client indicates a plan to harm someone else, practitioners are under duty to warn the affected party or contact peace officers. Stating the limitations of confidentiality at the outset helps clients know exactly what to expect from their practitioner. In the previous instances, the practitioner would, of course, best assist the client by first helping him to consider his choices in light of legal requirements and encouraging him to take the required action. In my experience, working with clients to encourage them to take needed steps such as notifying relevant agencies is the best route and allows for mutual consent regarding legally mandated breaches of confidentiality.

Permissions

As suggested, frequent checking in with clients about their responses to any planned or given intervention is advisable. Obtaining client feedback builds rapport, shows clients you really care about their inner processes, and allows you as practitioner to adjust your responses and the treatment direction as needed.

Touch is an especially sensitive issue for most people in distress. Many people have experienced touch in a negative way through either physical or sexual abuse. Much confusion also exists in our culture about the romantic, sexual overtones of touch, especially when given by an empowered person. Any touch other than a handshake needs clear permission from the client before it is given (unless you're a licensed massage therapist, physician, or nurse—in other words, in a licensed profession that requires touch to be effective).

Permission to treat is also important whenever you are requested to see a minor child or an elder who is under guardianship. Laws vary around the age of majority for children (anywhere from twelve to eighteen years of age), so parental consent is the best way to ensure permission. If the parents are divorced, there may be a difference of opinions about energy therapies, so make sure you have agreement from both parties. In institutional settings, it is additionally a good policy to explain your method to the staff person in charge so that there is no confusion or mistrust when you administer energy treatments.

Example of a First Session to
Set Mutual Agreements in the Therapeutic Contract

To bring to life our discussion of these energy care principles, let's consider an example of a first session with a new client to demonstrate how an ethical practitioner, who is aware of accepted standards of energy practice, would engage the client.

Mindy is a counselor who meets with Judy for the first time. After Judy fills out a brief history and office forms, Mindy asks, "How are you feeling?"

Judy automatically replies, "I'm OK...." and hesitates.

Mindy notices her tight shoulders and stiff jaw. She also notes from the intake form that Judy wants to learn stress management for her challenging job and family life. Intuitively, Mindy senses that there is more to be known and asks, with concern in her voice, for specific information.

This time, Judy answers, "Well, I just had a close call on the freeway on my way here to see you. Someone missed me by a hair and I still feel quite shaky."

Brief trauma, such as a close call on the road can leave anyone out of sorts and imbalanced. Mindy knows that some of the many interventions she has learned for relieving bodily tension would be appropriate. She tells Judy that she would like to share some of the rebalancing methods she has learned and asks whether that would be agreeable with her.

"Sure," says Judy. "I need all the help I can get. I didn't realize until I got here how much that incident bothered me." She thanks Mindy for noticing and asks what, specifically, she will do.

Mindy explains, "I will ask you to sit in the recliner over here, and pass my hands over your field to notice where there is tension or congestion. Then I'll move my hands over the areas that seem most blocked to relieve pressure and hold my hands over each area at the end. Some people notice tingling or warmth, but please let me know any sensations you notice. Also, be sure to tell me if you feel any discomfort or have other questions."

Mindy goes on to explain that there are no known ill effects from the energetic approaches she will use, but that the immediacy of the incident on the highway may recede or fade. She also clarifies that Judy has the right to choose or decline whenever a method is suggested. She adds that there are many other methods she can describe that could also be helpful.

Judy thinks for a moment and responds, "What you explained sounds a bit unusual to me—but I'm sure it's better than taking a tranquilizer. I want to forget the terrible feeling of thinking I was going to be snuffed out by that idiot on the road!"

Both laugh a bit at Judy's verbiage about the incident as Judy relaxes into the chair. Mindy uses several interventions, asking Judy to breathe deeply, bringing an image of warmth to the parts of the body that feel tense, and then adds smoothing and modulating of her whole biofield.

Judy responds to the treatment by breathing more deeply and stating that she feels more confident to get out and drive again.

To complete the brief intervention, Mindy suggests that Judy allow herself to work with the breath and the imagery each morning, when in traffic, and when something disturbing happens. "Think of movements or positive self-statements you can make," she tells Judy. "You may not notice any dramatic changes right away other than increased well-being and a possible sense of inner calming. Like taking vitamins, these self-care actions will have a cumulative effect."

"I didn't know that I would have to do homework," Judy says. "I assumed that you would do something to me and that would be it."

Mindy and her client then discuss how an educational partnership will serve to empower Judy more than the passive approach of her just receiving treatments. Judy's wishes for the work are discussed and together they set goals for future sessions to increase Judy's ability to handle life stresses and decrease anxiety.

After Judy leaves, Mindy documents in the client notes that she explained informed consent including risks, benefits, and client choice, and records the interventions given, recommendations for client self-care, and the mutually set goals.

* * * *

The elements of the fiduciary relationship considered here set the stage for a positive healing relationship. Next, we'll explore how to select clients for energy therapy interventions to get the best results. Some people may be better served by other approaches because of their special needs.

CHAPTER NINE

CLIENT CONSIDERATIONS IN
ENERGY THERAPY INTERVENTIONS

I n my twenty years of consultation with energy therapy practitioners, I've noticed that many who are new to the energetic resources
for relieving human suffering go out with great enthusiasm to share
their skills. Often, relative novices choose skeptical or, even more challenging, cynical people for their first clients. Then, because things tend
not to work well with unreceptive people, the balloon of initial pride
bursts and the new practitioners become discouraged. Some even give
up attempting to share energy therapies. For this reason, it's important
for practitioners to remember two important tenets of the work: (1)
we share energy modalities in humility and remember that any healing responses come *through* us and not *from* us, and (2) we understand
the concept of nonattachment to outcomes, which means trusting that
our peaceful, caring intentions enable pure energy flow to bring about
meaningful effects in the client's body, mind, and spirit.

Having said that much, let's learn more about the kinds of clients
that can help your practice to thrive. Skeptics are persons who ask a lot
of questions and evaluate results for themselves, so healthy skepticism

is a good stance toward any new or unusual approach, such as energy therapy. Cynics, on the other hand, are people who deny the existence of anything they do not understand. Since Therapeutic Touch was the first energy modality to be introduced in Western medical settings, Therapeutic Touch received the most frequent attacks from large groups of cynics who still seem to delight in debunking methods that fall outside their established apertures of perception.

It is not a good idea to share a new endeavor with a cynic or someone who is not open to what you have to give. Hence, the need for full permissions, lots of client feedback, and practitioner discretion.

With due respect for all I've learned about energy therapies over the last thirty years, I still hold the stance of being a healthy skeptic. As a good scientist, I carefully observe my clients' responses to the interventions. Because the responses have, without exception, been positive for each client, I encourage and practice Healing Touch, energy psychology, and related energy therapies. I support your healthy skepticism as well and ask that you observe the results of your interventions when you engage your chosen energy modality.

It's wise to avoid overly skeptical or cynical people for your clientele. People with strong religious beliefs that eschew energy healing concepts or who are not open to thinking in a whole-person framework are likewise not good client candidates. Usually, it's unwise to choose family members as clients—unless you know that your relationship with them is basically healthy and balanced and you can remain unattached to the outcome. Experience has taught that family members' needs, especially in the emotional realm, can be quite overwhelming for most caregivers.

When I speak about energy therapies, people often ask me how they can help their spouse or family member who is unwilling, closed off, mentally unstable, or disturbed. My reply is simple: Don't. You are the partner or family member, not the therapist or professional. Someone you live with is not a good subject because on the emotional level you are so closely interconnected. If your partner is troubled, he or she needs professional help from a qualified person. Do, however, enjoy energy therapies for yourself and your supportive friends, especially as you begin your practice.

There are, indeed, many client considerations that must be understood to develop effective and fulfilling energy therapy practices. In addition to the ideas already mentioned, we must always:

- Be realistic about our scope of practice.

- Ensure that our clients are receiving adequate medical care and/or seeking other conventional resources.

- Know when to make a referral.

- Assess client willingness and ability to participate in energy modalities.

We'll explore each of these themes as they relate to setting professional standards for the practice you have created and wish to maintain as a valued participant in your community.

Defining Your Scope of Practice

Your personal scope of practice is based on realistically assessing your degree of knowledge, skill, and experience. This also means you have self-awareness and insight into your strengths and weaknesses. For example, you may determine that you really enjoy working with children of a certain age group, or that you prefer helping more seasoned adults. Some helpers enjoy and appreciate strong-willed people; others find that they generate too much emotional turmoil. These preferences can help you shape how you present and market to potential clients and select the clients you could best help. Knowing your limitations can also help you define the referral sources you need to achieve best outcomes for your clients.

Scope of practice for licensed practitioners means working within the framework of the license they hold. One important scope of practice consideration is that only nurses, physicians, and massage therapists have the right to touch as part of their professional standard of care and licensure. All other licensed healthcare professionals need to ask patient or client permission to touch the body even when the client is fully clothed. In the case of unregulated practices such as energy therapies, careful attention to client permissions for any action, especially touch, must be obtained prior to extending touch.

Ensuring That Conventional Medical Care Is Present

As energy therapy professionals, we recognize that we're practitioners of a nonconventional perspective that operates from a different frame of reference, or paradigm, than conventional modalities. The theoretical base holds the reality of the human energy system, something as yet unseen except with the most recent measurements of subtle energies. Research additionally shows many energy therapies to be effective in providing pain relief, trauma release, anxiety reduction, and deep relaxation. But neither theory nor present research is totally conclusive—and energy therapies are not yet fully accepted within mainstream healthcare.

Our enthusiasm, however, may blind us to the need for conventional forms of care to benefit our clients. Failure to ensure, for instance, that clients have received adequate medical evaluation and care can result in significant legal liabilities.

Attorney Midge Murphy writes:

> Whether you are a licensed or unlicensed healthcare provider, clients could make a malpractice claim against you for not receiving adequate conventional care during their treatment with you. This is a civil action in which clients could assert that not receiving medical assistance while under your care caused them injury. If you are...licensed, a malpractice claim by a client could also trigger professional discipline action by your state's licensing board....[for] practicing below the established standard of care.[1]

Considering conventional treatments is an essential part of the professional plan of care we develop with clients. Client reports of unspecific pain, for example, may be related to a blocked flow of energy, but it can also be indicative of blood vessel constriction, nerve irritation, or an unidentified tumor. Thus any physical pain must be assessed by a physician or medical provider who is qualified to rule out the presence of a medical condition. Similarly, attention deficits, such as scattered thinking, inability to concentrate, and free-floating anxiety—symptoms that can often be relieved with biofield balancing exercises—could also be related to neurological dysfunctions or undiagnosed adult attention deficit disorder, both of which would require careful assessment and treatment by a neurologist.

Emotional pain is similarly related to many causes, not only energy system imbalance. For example, depression is well known to be related to emotional upheavals and/or unresolved anger, but it can also be caused by early onset of an undetected physical condition. Diabetes in its early stages, for example, is marked by depression, anxiety, and "lows" due to blood sugar deficits.

An essential standard of care in energy therapies is to ensure and document that adequate medical assessment of client symptoms has occurred. Often, clients seek energy caregivers when they have exhausted conventional medical or psychological care. Several factors may have been at work: (1) the client did not know what specialty he should seek for his condition; (2) clients may not wish to use allopathic medicine, with its tendency to rely solely on chemical and surgical interventions; (3) the client may have encountered physicians who said, "I cannot help you further," or "Come back when your symptoms are worse to make a definitive diagnosis."

Perceptive practitioners will do their best to find out what is bringing the person to seek their care and obtain a full history of medical and psychological treatments received. Astute caregivers will note patterns of injury that recur, although there may have been differing diagnoses given each time. Energetic symptoms also often precede the actual outbreak of disease, and an intervention can cause energetically blocked areas to release and resume a healthy flow of *qi*. Symptoms may diminish or disappear altogether. Just the same, if the client has not received a physical examination within the past year, it's wise to make sure a medical examination is made as soon as feasible.

What is the energy practitioner's responsibility if the client refuses the conventional medical or psychological care you recommend? In most states, it is required that anyone who charges a fee for services and presents herself as a professional must document the fact that adequate medical evaluation has been strongly recommended. Even unlicensed practitioners need to do their utmost to prevent charges of negligence or malfeasance by including conventional care in their treatment planning.

Client refusal is an opportunity to be resourceful and creative. Practitioners need to discuss such an ethical and professional standards dilemma openly with the client. Sometimes a significant other of the client's can be included in the discussion to help bring support to your stance. At other times, you may be able to identify a professional who would be acceptable to the client, such as a holistic health physician. An extreme solution would be to refuse to give continued care to the person who does not comply with your stated need to meet the ethical and legal requirement of medical supervision. Another acceptable option would be to obtain an express written legal statement that defines the client's "assumption of risk" for his own health.[2]

The partnership between caregivers and consumers of services is vital. Our part of the therapeutic contract is to make the highest quality of care available. This is especially true in cases that exceed our expertise and scope of practice. Referral to appropriate specialists is also part of effective treatment planning and is discussed further in chapter 12. Together the healer and healee are partners in seeking the best sources for presenting problems and the many factors involved in finding resolution of distress.

Assessing Client Willingness to Participate in Energy Therapies

Some people assume that they know what energy therapies can achieve because they have heard about results from friends. They may also be responding to a fad in their community or be fascinated with the mysterious quality that the work seems to engender. Informed consent is therefore essential not only for clients who are new to energy concepts, but also for those who seem well versed but may have limited perceptions or unrealistic expectations.

Assessing the true willingness of clients to receive our services with realistic expectations is essential in determining if a given treatment modality will actually fit with specific client needs. Despite the wide applicability of energy methods for many physical and emotional issues, skilled practitioners need to move beyond thinking that "one size fits all." Some individuals may not be ready for the nonverbal aspect of the work or the increased focus on self-care and insight we espouse. Biofield interactions create an intimacy that may well be too intense for some people or generate dependency issues in others. Practitioners and clients have heightened sensitivities to each other that may seem quite foreign to clients used to talk therapies. Additionally, the concept of energetic practices may seem strange even to the client who has stated the desire to experience a specific modality you offer. Practitioners need to evaluate carefully the clients' abilities to integrate energy interventions into their daily lives and family structures, especially if they live with family members who are dramatically opposed to energy healing.

Correct use of power is a central issue, as clients are suggestible due to the power differential in all therapeutic relationships. More than in traditional cognitive therapies, clients experiencing energy modalities tend to have increased absorption of subtle innuendos. Patients with severe physical or emotional pain will try almost anything for relief. Clients may interpret practitioner's positive experience with others to mean they will be free of their distress without doing the personal work they may need to do.

Careful assessment of clients is important to avoid later pitfalls. One principle to remember: the more disempowered the client is, the more care should be taken in introducing any innovative technique.

Here are some sample questions to help you evaluate client responsiveness before engaging a client in an energy-oriented treatment:

1. How does the person relate to you?

2. Is there a sense of openness and willingness to learn?

3. What is the level of self-insight?

4. Is there willingness to learn self-care?

5. Is the person willing to do homework and report back?

6. Is the person able to set realistic goals?

7. Is the person willing to accept referral to other practitioners as needed?

8. Is the individual willing to give feedback?

9. Will the client endeavor to correct any misunderstandings?

10. Is the person engaged in a lawsuit or other action that may prevent him from really wanting to get better?

Everyone is different, and often the stated reason for seeking you as a practitioner may be quite different from hidden or unconscious ones. Your care in assessing clients will help discern the people who are seeking an adventure, or a parental figure, rather than wanting positive change in their lives. When you have doubts or are not sure, it's helpful to teach one sample method you can safely offer and then pay attention to the person's response to the new information. It can be hazardous simply to jump at the opportunity to treat all comers, especially in light of possible psychological disturbances and hidden agendas.

Matching Energy Interventions to Client Needs

One of the greatest criticisms I've heard of energy therapy practitioners is that they do not have established criteria for selecting appropriate clients or for matching clients to effective interventions. Put simply, many practitioners assume everyone can benefit from the methods they have learned. Although it is true there is value in relaxation and in being in the comfort of a healer's presence, the diabetic really does need blood sugar regulation, the person with a deformed hip really needs an orthopedist, the adult attention deficit disordered client may benefit from medication, and pain of unknown origin always needs full medical evaluation. In a similar vein, people with emotional anxiety may respond well to energetic interventions, but underlying trauma often requires more in-depth psychotherapy. Chemically addicted people need the contributions of numerous skilled approaches in addition to what energy therapies can offer.

Ideal clients for energetic intervention are individuals who demonstrate the following characteristics:

- Intact ego structure with good self-esteem and sense of personal identity.

- Clear intention for positive change.

- Interest in energy therapy and willingness to participate in the learning process.

- Ability to set, understand, and maintain boundaries.

- Accepting and honoring the stated therapeutic contract with mutually set goals.

- Willingness to evaluate progress and give feedback.

- Recognition that other practitioners and referral sources may be needed.

With these qualities present as they enter the therapeutic relationship, clients also learn that the very interaction between facilitator and seeker is part of the healing process. Healthy relationships with clients result in a transformational process in which every aspect of the client—physical, emotional, mental, and spiritual—can become enhanced in new ways. In contrast to more conventional concepts of curing, where symptom relief is regarded as the ultimate outcome and the client is a passive recipient, healing within the new paradigm of energy therapy is a participatory venture in which caregiver and client collaborate to find the best insights and outcomes possible.

Having listed the qualities that are desirable, we can also identify the client qualities that would cause us to be very cautious. Some persons are inappropriate for energetic interventions because other work needs to be done first. Others may benefit more from learning self-care exercises or working with different approaches. Warning signals for practitioners to note are:

- Poor reality contact; the person does not seem to be oriented to space and time or boundaries; lack of a clear train of thought.

- Being scattered or confused, with poor recall.

- Being suspicious or misinterpreting what is said.

- Presence of severe systemic interferences, such as untreated pain, allergies, environmental sensitivities, chemical imbalances, dissociative states, or addictions.

- Confusion about touch, with a tendency to romanticize the caregiver.

- Presence of long-standing personality disorders, often evidenced by going to many therapists, being litigious, or consistently finding fault with others.

- Setting unrealistic expectations without self-insights.

- Forming excessive attachments; high dependency needs.

- Unwillingness to engage in treatment planning or following referral suggestions.

Although this list is by no means exhaustive, it identifies areas for concern. The proverbial ounce of prevention is worth a pound of cure—caution and willingness to refer clients who do not fit your scope of practice or personality style will save lots of grief later. An unhealthy relationship often becomes frustrating and potentially harmful to both parties. While I as a psychotherapist with many years of experience might feel I have something to offer from an energetic perspective to people with several of the issues listed, I would do so only with great caution and frequent consultation. Better yet, I would want such people to connect with practitioners who have more expertise in their area of need.

Some clients seek energy practitioners because they are disinclined to take their prescribed medications. Patients with brain chemistry imbalances, such as schizophrenia and bipolar disorder, are best maintained with carefully monitored medical protocols within currently known standards. Energy-oriented caregivers may be able to help these individuals to learn self-care exercises and to find ways of making peace with their diagnoses.

We need, however, to tread very lightly around the accepted medical treatment protocols that are allowing such patients to lead fairly normal lives. If a suggestible client were to sense a practitioner's lack of support for an established medical treatment, she might cease taking needed medications. Another complication is that the effects of ceasing psychotropic medications may not become evident until several months later since many of the positive blood effects established by using the prescription drop only gradually and imperceptibly at first. Side effects from withdrawal may actually be more severe than the patient's initial symptoms and suicidal ideation can become elevated.

We need to remind ourselves that there are no quick answers to the complex issues in some clients' lives. Above all, we operate within the ethical standard of avoiding harm to clients.

Being Aware of Client Issues Beyond One's Scope of Practice

No one person can meet all the needs of a given client. Thus all experienced caregivers and advanced practitioners develop a list of effective referral sources. For example, massage therapists need to be ready to refer clients for deeper emotional therapy when repeated or painful memories surface while they are receiving physical touch.

Since many clients seek energy practices in efforts to avoid the limiting parameters of conventional medical methods, practitioners can further serve their clients and community by becoming acquainted with holistic physicians or allied healthcare providers with prescription privileges to whom they can refer clients. In addition, anyone in practice needs to know good referral sources in other professions, such as social work, home care, massage, or hospice care so that when the need arises, they have a variety of such providers readily available.

The ongoing questions in every therapeutic relationship are: Have I done what other practitioners would do to meet my duty to help the client? Have I acted in any way that could be considered negligent (an act of omission)? Have I done anything that could be considered malpractice (an act of commission)?

Seeking effective referral sources is thus a practical standard of professional care. Failure to refer would be considered an act of omission while referring to someone incompetent or inadequately trained would be an act of commission. Both are potential issues to the unwary and can greatly harm the public image of energy therapy practitioners in their communities, as we'll explore further in chapter 12.

* * * *

So far, we've discussed many aspects of practitioner awareness in client relationships. In the next two chapters, we'll look at less usual but pertinent client realities: the possibility of nonordinary states of consciousness and the activation of primal archetypes. Both are client experiences that are likely to occur when receiving energy modalities and practitioners need to be able to respond appropriately.

Chapter Ten

Addressing Clients' Nonordinary States of Consciousness

W e've discussed how the intimate nature of biofield inter-connections and centered intentions for clients intensify the therapeutic relationship. We've also come to recognize the many areas of client vulnerabilities associated with their physical and emotional distresses. Because clients can often be susceptible to suggestion, we as practitioners must frequently and carefully explain informed consent and check for permissions.

Another context in which the practitioner must possess skill and competence is in recognizing and addressing the unusual states of consciousness that may occur quite spontaneously with energy therapies, especially when clients develop deeper levels of transference and trust. Most people's awareness changes when they are listening to a friend or caregiver, but shifts in consciousness are likely to be amplified and unusual within the context of energy therapies. This is due to the more intimate nature of the work as well as its nonverbal and somatic aspects. Clients relax and breathe more deeply than they would in talk therapy or medical settings. Because disconnection from bodily sensations is so prevalent in our culture, receiving an energy treatment may connect the client to himself in novel and often unusual ways. Fear and distrust of connecting to one's deeper being may surface unless the helper is prepared to address effectively whatever emerges from within the client.

While doing self-care with energy methods, clients may additionally access unusual levels of understanding. Homework practices, such as tapping meridian acupoints, repeating an affirmation or mantra, rubbing neurolymphatic reflex points, holding or rotating the chakras, or balancing oneself through meditation and imagery can bring some clients to different, unknown levels of consciousness.

In the past, psychologists researched altered states of awareness during drug treatments and the use of mood-changing substances. They also developed techniques to assist client self-insight through such methods as hypnosis, intensive meditation practices, guided imagery, breathwork, inner child work, and age regression. Each of these methods requires extensive training and experience for psychotherapists to reach proficiency. The intention of each of these approaches is to facilitate emotional breakthroughs for clients who cannot find relief from suffering through more traditional means, such as cognitive behavioral therapies.

For our discussion here, I want to focus on the nature of spontaneous shifts in consciousness that can occur in an energy-oriented session and the practice considerations that must be addressed, even though most energy practitioners do not have the additional competencies mentioned. These spontaneous and often very powerful events occur quite differently from the intentional, skilled used of psychotherapeutic methods. For one, they can happen unexpectedly without the caregiver's or client's intention or choosing. Additionally, addressing them within the relationship built on trust requires practitioners to stretch beyond usual ways of knowing.

I'm calling these unexpected events "nonordinary states of consciousness," following Kylea Taylor's valuable standards for practice.[1] Nonordinary states of consciousness can range anywhere from mild trance to very deep shifts in perception. They are especially likely to occur in sessions in which the client is comfortable with the practitioner and is willing to let everyday perceptions recede. Nonordinary consciousness includes a wide range of phenomena, such as daydreaming, reverie, deep concentration, losing track of time, "spacing out," dissociating from the present, having biographical flashbacks, reliving past trauma, activating emotionally charged imagery, experiencing emotional flooding, feeling intense energy releases, experiencing out-of-body states, sensing contact with angelic realms, and perceiving a sense of oneness with the cosmos.

What is our responsibility toward these client events? How do we address client disbelief or fears that may accompany the experience? A central standard of care is to bring helpful empathy to such a setting and to assist clients in reframing their internal experience as a possible significant breakthrough and learning experience. Supporting the client's process means helping her to see emotional discharge or an unusual event without judgment or limiting perception and assisting her in integrating what has happened for her personal development and growth.

Maintaining a healthy, healing relationship with the client who has nonordinary experiences requires us to be cognizant of the many possible states of consciousness and to be prepared to assist clients with acceptance. Clients often think they've gone crazy or have "lost it" when shifts in consciousness happen. They may feel quite embarrassed or vulnerable when something unexpected occurs, so it's our task to help define these events as positive, transformative incidents that are a natural part of self-discovery.

Nonordinary states of consciousness are more likely to arise in one-on-one sessions, but I've experienced a large variety of these states in workshop classes that involved practice exchanges among participants. One such event occurred with a nurse who told the whole group afterward in shocked disbelief, "I hope you don't think I've gone off my rocker, but I saw my father who has been dead for ten years just now while my partner helped me to relax and balanced my field." It was a great relief for her to know that receiving the image was all right and natural. In addition, I suggested that it could be a healing connection for her. At that suggestion, she cried softly and told the group how much she had always wanted to be loved by her father who had often seemed distant and aloof. His coming to her in the reverie allowed her to know that he loved her. As often happens, several class members wanted to chip in, give advice, and share their own related father stories. At that precious moment, it was most important to hold respectful silence. After a few minutes, she smiled and said, "Thank you for listening." For the rest of the weekend workshop, she was a happy and changed person: her perception of herself as someone so loved by her father that he would appear to her from beyond the veil of death gave her a deep sense of fulfillment.

Understanding Many Forms of Consciousness

In our materially oriented culture, many people have come to believe there is only one reality: the tangible, everyday consensus reality that is perceived through the five senses. The presence of the less tangible worlds of emotions, inner processing, intuition, spiritual connecting, and dreams indicates that human beings are capable of much more than sensory perceptions. Almost any thinking person who is aware of a reflective self will begin to access other forms of consciousness.

Human consciousness is actually an expanding continuum that extends from day-to-day awareness to mild reverie and to deeply unify-ing states. Knowing which aspect of the continuum is present in clients allows practitioners to track their inner states and respond appropriately. The person in ordinary awareness will have his eyes open, speak easily, hold a correct sense of time, and be cognizant of surroundings. Someone in a mild state of nonordinary consciousness will appear thoughtful, focused on his inner process of recalling the past or envisioning the future. He will still be able to respond to questions and return to the present readily.

The client in a deeper altered state of awareness will appear to be in a trance, unable to express himself verbally, and have difficult shifting back to the here and now. In this state, if there is adequate support and acceptance, the client may move to deeper internal levels of self, express himself through bodily movement or voice tones rather than speech, and discover mystical or transpersonal realms. The physical body may be very still and relaxed with occasional deep breathing, fluttering eyelids, and paling of the skin, most noticeably around the mouth. There may also be regression to other times in history or moments of intense emotional abreaction. The person's whole frame of reference and sense of self may be changed during, and possibly after, the experience.

Table 10.1 Continuum of Major Levels of Consciousness

Caregiver's external perception of client	Ordinary, everyday awareness	Mild reverie	Deep, nonordinary consciousness
Eye movements	Eyes open	Eyes relaxed or closed	Eyes closed, flickering eyelids as if seeing images
Speech pattern	Speaks easily	Thoughtful, few words, internal imagery	Unable to speak, expression through movement or sounds
Sense of time	Accurate sense of time	Inwardly focused, some time distortion	Strong time distortion, as if in a dream or another location
Awareness of surroundings	Present in the here and now	Able to respond to questions	Difficulty shifting back to the present

Perceptive practitioners will allow plenty of time and supportive silence for the client who is in deeper levels of nonordinary consciousness by respectfully standing aside and holding positive intention for the inner work. The role of the caregiver shifts from guiding interactions to "holding the light" of safety and trust, allowing the space for the client's inner processing. Toward the end of the session, caregivers may speak gentle reminders to return to the present so there is ample time to debrief anything that the client wishes to share and to integrate insights. Further, the practitioner needs to ensure that the client is fully alert and able to give address, telephone number, and/or date and to transport himself safely from the protected setting of the session.

Educating Clients about Possible Nonordinary Experiences

Conscientious discussion of the possibility of nonordinary states with clients is best done early in the caring relationship. Since practitioners cannot ignore the presence of such events, we must do as much as we can to prepare clients and to normalize unusual experiences for those who trust in our care. Most practitioners of energy therapies are already themselves on a path to wider aspects of consciousness, so seeking understanding of these possibilities is quite natural.

Some of the finest minds of the twentieth century have helped to describe maps of various levels of human consciousness. Psychologist Carl Gustav Jung was a pioneer in charting paths into the unknown terrains of the subconscious mind with his extensive studies of indigenous cultures and the hidden workings of his own mind and dreams.[2] Psychiatrist Stanislav Grof, cofounder of holotropic breathwork, is another hero who explored deeper terrains of the human mind.[3] Anthropologist Mircea Eliade researched the many unusual forms of perception in extensive cross-cultural research,[4] while Ken Wilber has written extensively about the transpersonal domains and summarized his learning into a brief history of everything.[5] Reading the work of these leaders will enhance practitioners' perceptions of the vast possibilities that can emerge from a healthy human psyche.

"Inner space travel" is the phrase that captures for me the vast domains of our own minds. These terrains are much less investigated and catalogued than the surface of the moon or undersea geography. Proceeding with our own explorations of inner space will give us greater appreciation of the areas that clients may encounter on their journeys to self-actualization.

Nonordinary states are not pathological but rather a natural part of human maturing. The states we're discussing here differ markedly from the defensive patterns that function to hold in or repress subconscious material. They in no way resemble the fixations, bizarre hallucinations, and irrational patterns that relate to disturbed brain chemistry. In contrast, nonordinary states occur when clients are at ease enough to let down their defenses and open to further understanding of themselves. Unusual states may signify readiness to grow emotionally, to stretch the apertures of consciousness, to become more fully alive—they need to be welcomed, just as an interesting dream image would be welcomed.

Some of the nonordinary states I'll describe here may seem strange to the reader who has not had a personal experience with them. Other practitioners will have seen in their long-term practices several of the unusual perceptional states listed here. They are:

- Dissociation from the present; time distortion.

- Reliving a traumatic event.

- Reexperiencing biographical material.

- Perceptions of traveling out of the body.

- Having spiritual visions.

- Reliving one's birth trauma.

- Intense releasing of bodily energy in spasms, known as *kriyas*.

- Recalling dramas that occurred in human history.

- Remembering a past life.

- Connecting with angels or guides.

Psychological and neurological research is demonstrating the vast ability of the mind to change itself, to be highly flexible, and to connect with other energies in a nonlocal way.[6] Each of the phenomena listed is understandable as part of the further reaches of human nature.[7] Jung called the ability to reach into shared domains of consciousness the "collective unconscious" and posited that all of us are psychologically interconnected and capable of transpersonal perceptions. In trancelike states, clients can not only recall long-forgotten biographical events, but they can also feel connected to the pain of others who have suffered throughout human history. And, quite naturally, they can also experience the bliss of transpersonal, angelic domains.

Disconnection from the present happens very readily when clients feel safe—they know they do not have to speak, they can relax, and they feel comfortable with the caregiver. Along with this release of here-and-now concerns, clients may experience time distortion that leads to feeling that they have been resting for a long time even though only five minutes have passed, or thinking they have stayed with the practitioner for a few moments when in actuality an hour has passed. Explaining these possibilities ahead of time may well prevent recipients of energetic interventions from feeling they have been manipulated, that they are out of control, or that something is wrong with them. We can help normalize these events by stating they are possible and that there are no judgments attached. Instead, a good, neutral response from both parties would be to note simply, "How interesting."

Reliving a traumatic event may happen spontaneously and in the case of someone recently traumatized, it is part of his processing within the midbrain limbic system. Specific energetic techniques, like tapping meridian acupoints, can rapidly release repeated limbic response patterns. If the practitioner is not skilled in administering such a treatment, clients suffering from relived, severe trauma or flashbacks should be referred to a psychotherapist who knows how to facilitate relief as rapidly as possible.[8]

Continuing energetic interventions without methods to reduce distress can be retraumatizing if the pattern of emotional flooding becomes established whenever clients are in a relaxed state. Most therapists specializing in trauma release work will see clients for only the sessions needed so the support and care of the primary energy practitioner can continue.

Reliving biographical material, especially from childhood, may allow the client to complete an unfinished piece of history. This may include feeling the rage, helplessness, and fear associated with a specific situation.

Often, these memories indicate that further therapeutic work needs to be done. With the right kind of professional assistance, as mentioned regarding trauma, the client may be able to find resolution of dissociated parts of herself and return to happier, more functional participation in life.

Out-of-body experiences feel very strange to those who are not familiar with them. It is as if a part of the person's consciousness moves beyond the physical body to float above the body, look down at it and other people, or travel around a building or outside to another location. If this occurs, it's vitally important to help clients understand that they have a strong connection with their practitioner and that they can return back to the body and current reality any time they request it. A prior agreement as to a cueing word or touch is helpful. Out-of-body experiences may well be a signal of expanding client consciousness, but, if you're uncomfortable with clients who wish to explore this phenomenon further, referral to someone skilled in working with beyond- the-body experiences is in order.

The reliving of one's birth and possible related trauma enables clients to experience their body's first, most powerful imprint of the world around them. This experience may come in brief glimpses or unfold like a movie during an energy treatment session. The experience of fetal life before birth is usually very pleasant in contrast. Birth itself can be reprogrammed into a loving successful experience if the facilitator can guide the journey with helpful imagery.

It is certainly possible for clients to have spiritual visions when they move into deeper states of nonordinary awareness. The client may see and communicate with archetypal figures, a power animal, or a guiding angel. Such peak experiences are well described in the mystical literature of all major world religions. The person may find answers to existential issues and engage a new sense of purpose. There may be a sense of merging with the cosmos and spiritual unity.

Intense energy release phenomena can also occur. The literature from yogic traditions that date back many thousands of years describes these sensations as a rising of the *kundalini,* the core that moves energy from the lower chakras to the higher, more intuitive and spiritual centers. The energy release with this rising may cause a variety of somatic sensations, such as burning, sweating, feeling cold, and discomfort. It can be accompanied by uncontrollable shaking, jolts, and vibrations called *kriyas.* The releases may also be accompanied by seeing powerful images, lights, or colors and spontaneous crying, chanting, or toning.

Reliving dramas of human history can also occur. Usually and sadly, most of these are not pleasant memories from the collective human consciousness. As if in a dream, the client may access the terror of being burned at the stake, suffer on a slave ship, or feel physical abuse even though these are not part of his current biographical life.

Recalling a past life is usually even more specific than accessing a historical event. The full experience of another life in another place may unfold while the person is in a nonordinary state. Whether such a life actually occurred is not relevant because the most significant learning is the opportunity to explore the personal meaning for the individual. With skilled guidance, the past life can be explored more fully to connect with communication from the subconscious mind.

Most of these experiences can best be understood as an emergence of the client's soul into its full potential, which includes transpersonal, spiritual domains. When this is not understood by either the client or practitioner, there is a tendency to pathologize the experience and, by doing so, limiting its value. What may look like a spiritual emergency when seen through the lens of fear may, in reality, be a valuable spiritual emergence, an opportunity to become more fully oneself.[9] Practitioner presence with clarity, compassion, and acceptance for the client is essential. If the phenomena that occur with clients exceed your comfort zone or skills, referral is the logical choice, with care taken that the client does not interpret referral as rejection.

Expanded Definition of Informed Consent

As we can see from the brief discussion, the potential for occurrences of nonordinary states of consciousness and for learning from them is vast. It is as great as the human capacity to access expanded realms of the mind. For the energy practitioner without specific training in these areas, trusting the client's inner process is essential. Whenever you as a practitioner feel on uncertain ground, especially in dealing with nonordinary states of consciousness, the accepted standard of care is to seek consultation with a more knowledgeable practitioner.

That said, our understanding of informed consent has to broaden to include nonordinary experiences, especially as the therapeutic relationship develops. The intention of the practitioner is to demystify unusual states of mind by creating a climate in which fear and misperceptions can be avoided. The healthy flow of communication in the fiduciary relationship requires ongoing attention and careful monitoring.

Informed consent implies that the client knows what the therapist will do and how a procedure may affect him or her during and after the intervention. In the case of nonordinary states of consciousness, informed consent is different because of the difficulty in describing the experience before it has occurred and also because these states can arise unexpectedly. An expanded definition that better fits the situation of energy practitioners is cited by psychologists Pope and Vasquez as follows: "Informed consent is an attempt to ensure that the trust required is truly justified, that the power of the therapist is not abused intentionally or inadvertently, and that the caring of the therapist is expressed in ways that the patient clearly understands and desires."[10]

Practice Standards
in Relation to Nonordinary States of Consciousness

Some of the best ways to ensure healthy, healing relationships with clients who exhibit unusual phenomena are listed here as accepted standards of care within energy therapy practices:

- Accept the reality that some clients will have internal experiences that may be difficult to comprehend.

- Trust the client's process when there is a deep, trancelike state.

- In whatever way possible, accept and empower the client.

- Offer your neutral, nonjudgmental presence.

- Bring in the possibility of a positive focus to the unusual occurrence.

- Affirm the positive intention of the client's psyche toward growth and expansion.

- Avoid retraumatizing the client by helping him to reframe the experience.

- Practice only within your competence, your stated scope of practice, and refer or seek consultation for unusual client incidents or needs.

From an ethical perspective, practitioners must remember that when clients are undergoing nonordinary consciousness, they are more suggestible, less personally vigilant, and less able to speak for themselves than when in ordinary awareness. When client defenses are down, practitioner vigilance must increase since any comment or gesture could lead the client away from his own resources. At the same time, clients may experience stronger, more complex transference to the caregiver and want her advice or direction. Helpers need to walk a fine line from being a facilitator or guide to holding a safe space for the client's inner work.

Boundaries around touch also become blurred in the altered states discussed. Clients may need touch but not be able to ask for it; alternately, caregivers may sense touch is needed but are unable to get a direct answer. It's therefore a good idea to make agreements about nonverbal signaling either with a cue word the client will recognize, such as "help" or "be present," or by an agreed-upon touch on the client's body such as the hand or shoulder. Should the client feel distress during a nonordinary state, this mutual signal can be used by the practitioner to give comfort and to assist the client in returning to the present.

Shifts in consciousness are normal and occur for most people on a daily basis. In an energy therapy session, they may occur more frequently or with greater intensity. The sensitive practitioner accepts them as part of the dance of life and assists, comforts, and guides clients in these uncharted territories.

Closure and Ongoing Processing

Timing is an essential element in energy therapies, since we wish to make sure every client returns to alert, present-moment awareness before departing. One rule of thumb is to think of the sixty- or ninety-minute session time in thirds: the first third is for client check-in and self-report with ample time for mutual goal-setting; the second portion is the actual treatment time during which blockages are released to facilitate healthy flow of *qi;* and the third is a time for the client to debrief, share insights, integrate his experiences, and make sure he is in safe readiness to travel. Time is essential to tie up loose ends, ask questions, express emotional needs, and identify unresolved material that can be incorporated into planning for subsequent sessions.

Many clients continue to process in the times between sessions. Encouraging journaling, recording dreams, noting changes, capturing insights by writing or recording them, using affirmations, and repeating a self-care method that is helpful—all these are excellent ways to enhance the effectiveness of client learning so that their lives away from the caregiver genuinely improve. The more we as practitioners can help clients to participate in bringing energetic awareness into their lives, the more successful they will be.

For clients who have experienced nonordinary consciousness during a session, special care is advised. For one, they need to know when and how often the practitioner is available if reassurance or support is needed. Some deeper levels of consciousness may feel to clients like an internal emergency rather than an emergence of their being because they are groping in unknown territory. Feeling unprotected from the practitioner's care may foster the feeling of being lost and alone.

* * * *

The central professional standard of care in the presence of nonordinary consciousness states is to make sure clients feel safe and supported. The healthful, healing relationship can grow and expand when such care is consciously and diligently maintained and the caregiver herself is supported by knowledgeable professionals.

CHAPTER ELEVEN

THE SACRED CONTRACT BETWEEN CAREGIVER AND CLIENT

The ethic of caring and related standards of practice give us as energy therapy practitioners insight into ourselves and the special relationship we establish with our clients. One way of understanding this relationship is to see it as a sacred contract that may have formed within the collective consciousness of our vastly interrelated human lives.

In *Sacred Contracts: Awakening Your Divine Potential,* Caroline Myss gives energy caregivers psychospiritual tools for understanding the profession they've selected.[1] The personal sacred contract is the one practitioners create when choosing their calling, taking responsibility for their actions, making helpful choices, and understanding wise use of personal power. This agreement is made at the soul level, prior to conception and birth, and informs the lessons we chose in order to evolve spiritually.

Spiritual transformation comes about when individuals begin to comprehend events around them as part of the larger plan for their lives. Myss writes: "As vital parts of a larger, Universal Spirit, we each have been put here on earth to fulfill a sacred contract that enhances our personal spiritual growth while contributing to the evolution of the entire global soul."[2] Part of our contract requires that we discover our true calling and the Divine, in turn, promises to give us guidance, through intuition, coincidences, dreams, nonordinary states of consciousness, and other indications. The sacred contract also appears to reach out to seekers so that we can work with them easily and provide the very resources they need.

Myss developed her theory after many years of working as a medical intuitive, "reading" the energy of people in distress, and working closely with Norman Shealy, MD, founder of the American Holistic Medical Association. Most people, she discovered, want to know their purpose in life because finding meaning supports health and vitality. Deviating from the path the soul has chosen can create illness, frustration, and disharmony in the personal energy system. This appears to be the organizing principle in each person's unique contract with Creation.

When we frame our relationships with clients in energy healing practices as a spiritual contract, we quite naturally seek ethical behaviors and higher standards of care. We learn to honor the interconnections with our clients and to create right, healthy relationships with them. Reverence for the web of life in all its many forms is also included as part of the practitioner's personal journey.

Ethical behavior means acting with integrity. This means the caregivers' behaviors are congruent with their values, knowledge, intuition, and feelings. It also means that there is harmonious, consensual dialogue within them that guides external actions that are consistent and positive. Acting in accordance with their personal sacred contract guides practitioners to honor the unique, caring covenant with each of their clients.

The standards of care that emerge from this awareness go far beyond moral codes and laws, which may change with different times and cultures. Spiritual truths do not vary. When we see our relationship with clients as a sacred agreement, we are invoking spiritual truth as the governing force. This allows both parties to touch into deeper awareness of their values and their soul's purpose.

Archetypes as Guides to Awareness in Helping Relationships

The concept of human archetypes was popularized by psychologist Carl Jung to understand patterns that have repeated themselves throughout human history and are present in the unconscious mind of the individual.[3] Archetypes are prototypes or examples of an original model or pattern that is shared by many people's thoughts and emotions, across cultures and nationalities. They also serve as universal symbols of cosmic intelligence and dynamic living forms of energy. Archetypes define the structure of our lives and speak to us in symbolic language. Mother, for example, is an archetype that is repeated and revered throughout human legacies as symbolic of the caring nurturing pattern of unconditional love.

It's important to remember, though, that archetypes are neutral and manifest energetic patterns of both light and dark. An integral part of this insight is for individuals to recognize and understand their shadow aspects so that integration can occur. The Mother archetype can thus also relate to controlling patterns of pushing, directing, and limiting, while protecting and defending the young at all costs—a less glamorous but very real part of many people's experience with their parents.

Jung believed that archetypes live in the collective unconscious realm where all people are interconnected. He was the first to explore extensively the nature of universal archetypes in human consciousness. Work with archetypes shows that they are patterns of influence that come alive as part of the individual's personality. Knowledge of these patterns helps us understand why we take on certain tasks and relationships even though they seem burdensome or destructive.

In energy healing practices, archetypes are much more prevalent due to the intensive and often unconscious levels of the sharing. Sessions frequently move beyond the biographical realm into intuitive and transpersonal domains. Archetypes therefore become amplified and form an integral part of the healing process.

Although many different interpretations of archetypes are possible, we'll focus on Myss's essential orientation here. When she developed her concept of the sacred contract in her studies of Jung's archetypes, she concluded that each person has a unique combination of twelve archetypes that underlie the personality. The number twelve relates to symbolic and mystical qualities that have held cross-cultural meaning for millennia, as in twelve houses of the zodiac, twelve months of the year, and twelve hours on the clock.

Four of the archetypes are universal energy patterns we all share for survival, while the other eight are unique to each person. Part of the challenge in discerning our sacred contract is to conduct personal reviews to determine which of the over eighty possible archetypes are most active. Myss identified four major life patterns, which all people develop in order to survive in the physical world: the Child, the Victim, the Prostitute, and the Saboteur. All four of these basic patterns influence our relation to power, decision-making, and authority figures.

Being aware of the four principal archetypes can assist helpers in understanding the dynamics of their own inner process, as well as those of clients. For practitioners, the survival archetypes need to be known and stabilized to create safety in the clear decision-making that supports clients' highest good. Implementing the highest standards of care flows from this maturing and insight.

The other eight archetypes, unique to each personality, may be described as ancient figures—Goddess, Warrior, King, Magician, Scribe—or as contemporary ones, such as Networker, Environmentalist, Change Agent, Cheerleader, or Protester. When practitioners become fluent in seeing these patterns in themselves and their clients, they can understand the nature of therapeutic interactions more fully.

The Survival Archetypes

The patterns linked to survival mechanisms serve as guardians of healthy, positive healing endeavors. Described briefly, their key purposes are:

- The Child is guardian of innocence and assists the caregiver in honoring the capacity for joy and connecting with the Inner Child of others.

- The Victim guards against being victimized, reminding practitioners to steer away from activities that diminish their energy and strength.

- The Prostitute reminds helpers to protect against prostituting themselves by holding clear values, standards of care, and honoring their talents and abilities.

- The Saboteur ensures that helpers will not harm or sabotage themselves by carefully weighing choices and avoiding reliance on emotional whims.

The Child

The Child archetype is guardian of innocence and thereby is one of the most powerful patterns. It represents our fundamental, first stage of consciousness. Popular self-help literature gives many examples and variations to the Child archetype, including the Wounded Child, the Magical Child, the Needy Child, the Natural Child, and the Inner Child.

Since the power differential is inherent in all therapeutic relationships, awareness of the Child archetype helps us understand the client as the more vulnerably party in the therapeutic relationship. The implicit acknowledgment that the practitioner has more knowledge than the client is often amplified due to clients' physical distress or emotional pain and to the intuitive aspects inherent in energy modalities. Because of the power differential, clients often respond to their therapist as they would to people in authority or even to parental figures. Unresolved childhood issues may come into the relationship because of unconscious issues. Professional healing relationships usually have strong transference in which the Parent/Child archetypes can easily become reactivated.

Thus, needs, feelings, and issues from childhood can be projected onto the helper as a parent figure. Practitioners who are aware of the dynamics of the client's Child archetype will be able to maintain clear boundaries and distinguish client material from their own. In addition, practitioners will know that creating a safe, sacred place for meetings is an essential standard of care. Ideally, practitioners honor their own Child patterns by respecting their needs for play, creativity, and joy.

The Victim

The Victim archetype is the guardian of personal self-esteem and self-care. Being abused or taken advantage of is a common concern and this archetype helps caregivers be alert to potential misunderstandings in clients. The archetypal pattern reminds us to empower ourselves and take responsibility for our well-being.

Awareness of the Victim also helps practitioners notice when they shift to sympathizing excessively with clients. For example, a therapist who has a strong longing to be a magical healer may welcome the client's attribution of change to his great skills. In such a case, the client loses a sense of her own accomplishments and insights—in short, she becomes a victim. Codependency can further feed client helplessness and lack of self-esteem.

The caregiver may inadvertently step into the archetypal pattern described by psychotherapist Steve Karpman as the Drama Triangle.[4] There are three interchangeable roles within this Drama Triangle—the Rescuer, the Victim, and the Persecutor. If the therapist sees herself as a Rescuer, then the client automatically becomes a Victim, the "one-down" person. The client may discount his own wisdom and project unusual powers onto the caregiver. In addition, the client is betrayed by thinking the caregiver did his healing work. Such betrayal, failing to help clients to identify their own work, quietly puts the caregiver into the Persecutor role. The client may realize at a later time that the therapist did not act in his best interest and switch to becoming a Persecutor by blaming the helper or bringing up ethics charges. Ultimately, the caregiver may end up as a Victim. Basically, no one wins.

By being aware of the Drama Triangle, caregivers can keep them-selves from jumping too quickly into trying to be an all-knowing

Rescuer. They also need to note whenever they feel compelled by a client's situation to extend beyond reasonable boundaries of good practice, such as offering to meet at unusual times, offering transportation, inviting clients to parties, lending money, and so on. Ethical practitioners always direct client appreciation back toward the client by saying, "This change came through your inner work, not mine. You are the author and director of the changes you choose."

When fully activated, the Victim archetype as guardian represents the strength of good boundaries and the helper's ability to see even the most distressed client as an empowered being. These parameters are essential for practitioners so they can be of highest service to their clients.

The Prostitute

The Prostitute archetype is the guardian of caregiver self-efficacy. The core issue is that we often sell ourselves short, prostituting ourselves, our values, our integrity, truths, mental abilities, even the soul—all for the sake of addressing real or imagined threats, such as financial insecurity. The Prostitute archetype is the ally who alerts us every time we consider moving away from our soul's purpose. An example of an active, negative Prostitute archetype is seen in someone who stays in a bad marriage or miserable job because she fears being alone or poor.

The client-facilitator relationship is rife with opportunity to engage the shadow side of the Prostitute pattern. For example, if the therapist continues to see a client only because she does not want to lose income, or because she gets an ego boost from having a prominent, adoring client, she is prostituting herself. The positive side of this archetype is engaged when the caregiver makes a clear commitment to put client needs and wishes ahead of his own. In that case, the Prostitute is the ally for honoring the sacred and ethical agreement between him and the person in need.

The Saboteur

The Saboteur archetype is the guardian of choices that support rather than harm. A core issue with this pattern is overcoming fear of change in one's life. The positive aspect of the Saboteur invites practitioners to act with courage and follow intuitive guidance in carefully considered increments. On the other hand, almost everyone knows the voice of their destructive, self-sabotaging tendencies. It is the voice that says we're not good enough, we don't have sufficient skill, we're incapable, and so forth. Most people also know what it's like to be sabotaged by others in relationships and the workplace.

The Saboteur, as guardian of choices, is highly active in the therapeutic relationship. Client change involves shifts in their view of themselves and relation to forces beyond their full understanding. Clients can experience emotional flooding, a greater sense of personal vulnerability, and disorientation since energy modalities create such significant openings to increased awareness.

The practitioner can use her position to provide permission to engage positive aspects, such as respect and courage, when clients feel hesitant or timid. We can also offer protection while clients explore new possibilities for themselves in the safe container of the helping relationship. Of course, knowing how and when to aid with permission and protection requires practitioners to have done their own work so they can be effective guides for clients traveling in uncharted, and sometimes frightening, new terrains.

Innovative energy modalities expand the framework of caring beyond clients' biographical domains to include the transpersonal. Archetypes reside within the transpersonal, the more than temporary domains. Thus archetypes are active participants in the healing relationship. In addition to the four major survival archetypes discussed so far, myriad other patterns or prototypes can impact the nature and scope of our client sessions.

Other Archetypes

In Myss's model, there are at least eight additional archetypes that influence the actions, feelings, and beliefs of each person. Observing, identifying, honoring, and working with our archetypes will enhance personal awareness and maturity as well as build foundations for appropriate, healthy, caring relationships with clients.

A predominant archetype that is prevalent among energy-oriented helpers is the Healer. This pattern manifests in those who have a passion for serving others to repair body, mind, and spirit. It expresses itself especially by choosing novel, innovative practices different from those traditionally associated with treating illness in institutional settings. Energy therapy practitioners are often strongly guided by this archetype to help clients release painful histories, and change their lives for the better. Myss states that the essential characteristic of this archetype is the ability to assist people in transforming their lives as well as being able to generate enough qi to channel and generate multidimensional change. Shadow aspects of the Healer archetype emerge when caregivers take advantage of those who need help or make claims beyond their actual abilities. Another failing of the Healer pattern is evidenced by an inability to take adequate care of oneself.

It is not uncommon for practitioners to believe fervently that they are Healers when, in fact, they hold the Rescuer or Servant archetype. Although the Rescuer may be helpful in intervening to help someone in distress, he often has difficulty keeping healthy boundaries and may fall into the Drama Triangle mentioned earlier.

The Servant archetype engages the person in genuinely wanting to help and benefit others at the expense of personal well-being. If this pattern resonates with you, it is essential to rededicate yourself to improved self-care (as elaborated in section II). Client needs can become totally consuming and cause practitioners to lose focus on essential priorities. Being overwhelmed by client needs can cause caregivers to overextend themselves and then actually dislike clients for being needy—a form of therapist countertransference.

In general, clients experiencing nonordinary states of consciousness have strong needs for touch, nurturing, and spiritual connecting. Potential for transference is great because of their deep desires and longings. Client may begin projecting archetypes of Mother, Father, Lover, Shaman, or Wizard, as their way of responding to the facilitator. The archetypal projections can range from the divine to the demonic. Unless careful preparation for nonordinary experiences is made (as discussed in the previous chapter), these projections can bring further confusion, boundaries issues, and discomfort to helping relationships.

A large number of varying archetypes can be active in therapeutic relationships. Practitioners who honor the sacred contract with their clients will be sensitive to patterns active in themselves and their clients. For example, the client may carry a Damsel archetype in which the client wants the caregiver to rescue her from distress and reward the Prince with romantic illusions. Savvy helpers will know to teach such clients that the relationship is not like the movies—it's about teaching her to become the catalyst for her own empowerment. Similarly, clients with the Slave archetype will need practitioners who encourage individual decision-making rather than following a leader.

A frequently seen practitioner archetype is known as the Judge. Knowing if you are prone to evaluate or pronounce judgments will help you allow the inner wisdom of the client to be the directing force of the healing process.

If either party, client or caregiver, carries the seductive archetype known as Don Juan, great attention has to be given to nuances, gestures, touch, or speech. The most frequent legal consequences come from blurred boundaries around sexuality. The healthiest standard of care is to understand that sex and romance are never in any way a part of the sacred, caring contract you make with clients.

Understanding the dynamic nature of archetypal patterns—both light and shadow—is an invaluable tool in handling the subtleties of energetic helping relationships. Openness in practitioners is a key factor in helping clients normalize their experiences even if they include archetypal patterns. Being present with an open mind is a key aspect in holding the light for the sacred contract and enables caregivers to accept archetypal myths as a springboard for learning and self-insight.

* * * *

As Mary Sykes Wylie states: "Blind allegiance to a particular therapeutic model becomes an ethical failing when the therapist consistently gives more weight to the model than to what the clients say they want and need."[5] Innovative energy modalities quite naturally expand the therapeutic paradigm beyond the client's biographical domain to include transpersonal experiences and nonordinary states of consciousness. It is our task as practitioners to learn and grow not only from client inner states, but also by expanding our own perceptive skills and talents.

VIGNETTES FOR SECTION III

Vignette III.1 The Drama Triangle Redux

Jessie was Ted's energy therapy client off and on over several years. She had benefited from his interventions and was enthusiastic about the ways working with acupoints and chakras enhanced her personal life. She brought her recent romantic partner, John, with her and asked Ted to help him as well.

Ted felt deeply gratified that Jessie sought him out to assist in her new relationship and quickly launched into several patterns that addressed the partner's blocked material. In this true example, the couple broke up several weeks later for a number of reasons, but the ex-partner sued Ted for "Using experimental methods with him that embarrassed him and resulted in alienation of affection from his girlfriend."

This is a good example of the Drama Triangle in action: (1) a request to assist the partner by Jessie who sees John as a Victim is made to the flattered therapist Ted who obliges by jumping into the Rescuer role; (2) John shifts to Persecutor by suing the therapist; (3) and the therapist becomes the Victim with a long lawsuit that actually resulted in having to give up his license to practice.

Discussion: Whenever you feel flattered or elevated by a client, step with great caution. What considerations would you need to make before seeing a client like John? (Think of informed consent, consensual contract, client selection criteria, and so on.)

Before jumping into such a seemingly innocent situation, you would need to consider that John is virtually unknown to the practitioner. What safeguards would you use to ensure that a new client is appropriate to energy-oriented approaches? How would you assess client readiness, interest, and willingness? The rules of informed consent and client choice are just as real, and more complex, when you're dealing with two individuals instead of one.

Vignette III.2 Here Comes the Judge

Sally was a well-respected practitioner in her community. Cyndi, another therapist, chose to work with her to resolve two complicated issues in her life. They had several sessions to establish rapport, which seemed primary to Cyndi. Sally was impatient to help get Cyndi's dilemmas resolved by using energy approaches.

Sally instituted energetic methods after three sessions, thinking there had been enough time for support and rapport. Cyndi felt overwhelmed by the whole process and the speed of changes. She failed to voice her concerns, however.

At the next session, Sally intuitively sensed something was amiss. She realized her Judge archetype had entered the situation by thinking Cyndi was ready for more intensive change than she actually was. Cyndi responded to Sally's judgments of her by feeling helpless and overwhelmed.

Sally also started to note how Cyndi's Victim and Saboteur archetypes were emerging by being pushed too quickly. Sally consciously chose to put her Judge on the back burner and to be fully present to Cyndi, accepting her and her need for stability and comfort. As Sally's positive Healer archetype emerged, both caregiver and client resumed their working relationship, which lasted longer and was more enduring and deeper than it would have been otherwise.

Discussion: In contrast to the previous vignette, the practitioner's awareness of archetypal patterns allowed her to curb her judgments and overzealous attempts to move the client forward. She allowed intuition to help her detect the subtle change in their relationship and then gently discuss client discomforts further. With the deepening trust that developed when the client acknowledged her Victim archetype and need for support, the practitioner was later able to use energy techniques with good outcomes.

Vignette III.3 History Becomes Too Alive

Kelly had developed a strong rapport with Joan and, as their work progressed, Kelly started sharing unusual dreams. Joan listened carefully and helped Kelly find positive meanings for herself. Joan also helped Kelly with physical pain and was able to help her find relief with biofield balancing methods.

Over time, Kelly started relaxing more deeply and went into trance. She returned from one trancelike state, looking bewildered and glancing around the room in fear. Joan was able to help her client reconnect to present reality with a mutually agreed-on gentle touch and by stating, "I'm here for you."

Kay described her inner vision of a dark cell from which she emerged to face a large crowd and have her head cut off. Her terror was palpable when she recounted the event. She tried to laugh it off as a wild dream, but Joan encouraged her to explore possible learning that could come from the reverie. Kelly then described the time and place of the event—it was like looking into a history book and being in the throes of the French Revolution for a short time.

As they considered the nonordinary state further, Kelly said she had no particular connection to the French Revolution other than, as a child, reading Victor Hugo's famous book *Les Miserables.* Neither Joan nor Kelly could attach any particular personal significance to the imagery, but they agreed that memories from the collective human unconscious can surface as intense culturally known incidents during nonordinary states of consciousness.

Kelly was relieved that Joan accepted her weird experience and helped to explore the context. It all came together for her a month later, when she attended the Broadway musical *Les Miz* based on Hugo's famous book. Without any pretenses, she was able to say, "I know a bit about the reign of terror." Her capacity for compassion and understanding of human depravity and redemption grew from experiencing the unusual state. The play became a real-life mirror of a terrible time in history and the tenacity of the human spirit.

Discussion: Although neither Kelly nor Joan could find a direct link to the trigger of the experience, they found something of value in the occurrence. Joan's insight to stay with her client by looking for possible connections and meanings empowered both of them to seek deeper wisdom rather than just discard the event as a wild dream. The psyche always has positive intentions in presenting a dream, a nightmare, a daytime vision, or a trance experience, and we can help clients to learn from themselves in powerful ways.

Vignette III.4 Avoiding Avoidance

Jake, a realtor with lots of stress, liked his energy sessions with Sam to relieve recurring anxieties. Sam combined energy therapy with massage and was able to establish a good working partnership with Jake.

During one very relaxing session, Jake began to recall childhood trauma of being kicked and then sexually assaulted. Thereafter, the visions grew stronger each time he visited Sam. Jake became so uncomfortable he stopped coming for therapy.

Sam knew something was amiss, although Jake had not shared any details. He asked his consultant and mentor what he should do. With the help of the consultant's input, he encouraged Jake to return so they could find the best path together. Although Jake was reluctant at first, the strength of his trust with Sam brought him to explain the problem. Once Sam knew the situation, he was able to refer Jake to a competent counselor who could release the trauma and allow for inner healing. Once Jake felt safe again within himself, he eagerly returned to Sam because Sam had proven himself to be a trusted professional with many resources.

Discussion: Rather than giving up or feeling rejected by Jake's avoidance, Sam made use of the two best resources any practitioner has—a consultant and a referral source. The healing relationship was able to continue with Sam's dedicated efforts to expand to resources beyond his skills as an energy-oriented massage therapist. Jake could have been one of the many clients who avoid facing their issues. The very thing he most needed—the support of a positive, objective caring relationship—would have been lost. Many clients wander from one practitioner to another without insight about what is really going on. Additionally, Sam was able to avoid the possible malpractice of doing psychotherapy without a license by enlisting the help of his consultant and the referral therapist.

Vignette III.5 Departure Without Comment

Clara was referred to Dora by a highly competent medical practitioner, Dr. J. Her presenting symptoms filled no identified medical diagnosis and yet Clara was steadily losing weight, and suffering from pain, insomnia, and bizarre nightmares.

Dora respectfully obtained a brief history from Clara, who expressed a desire to have her biofield balanced, as she it felt to be "full of holes." Dora explained the parameters of energy modalities, possible benefits and risks, and the client right to choose. She also clarified the limitations of confidentiality with the three exceptions she knew.

Clara was quite vague around committing to any treatment and complained about the fee she had agreed to over the phone. She did agree to participate in relaxation imagery so their session could end on a positive note. Dora wondered after Clara left whether she should call for a follow-up appointment or not. Trusting her intuition to wait, she contacted the referring physician directly after a week.

Fortunately, Dora had the presence of mind to have Clara sign the form that gave consent for Dora to speak with Dr. J. with respect to treatment planning. Once Dora recounted her experience with Clara, Dr. J. added a pertinent fact that she had not known before: Clara was plaintiff in a large lawsuit against her former employer for allegedly causing her too much stress. Clara's symptoms fit patterns of self-neglect, such as not eating or sleeping, possibly to create sympathies for the pending hearings. Neither of them ever heard from Clara again. She appeared to be seeking other practitioners to support the idea of getting a large settlement by making herself look pitiful.

Discussion: Few people can guess accurately what another person is truly about. Psychiatric disorders include patients who injure themselves for monetary gain or who set traps for practitioners so they can sue. This is why carefully setting boundaries, completing informed consent, setting mutual goals for increased functioning, and discussing limitations of confidentiality are so important at the outset. If someone does not want to get better for her own reasons, it is not the practitioner's responsibility to challenge those beliefs. Respecting clients' true wishes is sometimes difficult because we can see the potentials for improvement. Clients, I find, have a way of knowing when a practitioner is too honest and ethical to be fooled by vague requests or gamey tactics. They simply weed themselves out.

It's important to document both treatment and follow-up, especially in cases where there seems to be client nonparticipation. In the case of a litigious client, your client record is your best defense.

Vignette III.6 Client Needs Exactly What Is Rejected

Tina had a severe form of breast cancer that put her in repeated traumatic cycles of emotionally draining chemotherapy, hopeful remissions, and devastating recurrences. She came to her energy practitioner with one stated goal: "I want to feel better and have peace with my disease and my dying. Do *not* refer me to a physician. I hate them all!"

Jane, her practitioner, was concerned that she would be negligent if she did not include some form of conventional medical treatment in her care planning. She openly expressed her concern to Tina at their first session. After several meetings, Tina experienced relief from anxiety and developed a sense of connecting with her inner wisdom. Jane reopened the question of medical support when they had built sufficient trust and rapport. She mentioned two physicians whose practices included work for people in similar situations and who had exceptional compassion for people. The intention of referral was not only to make sure medical needs, such as pain management, were addressed but to make sure Tina received exactly the care that best supported her in her last days.

Tina evaluated each physician and actually ended up choosing a third who was recommended by her support group. For the rest of her life, which lasted about a year, Jane and the physician helped Tina to live without pain and to be effectively in charge of her end-of-life-care.

Discussion: This is another example of how being clear about your dedication to a good standard of care—the one of ensuring ongoing medical evaluation and support—helps to set the stage for successful outcomes. Helping clients through end-of-life care is one of the very powerful treatment options we can offer in energy modalities.

Vignette III.7 Passivity, Inc.

Denise was seventy-seven years of age and seemed to believe her doctors were saints. She was surprised and even miffed when Mary, her massage practitioner who incorporated energy modalities, suggested they set treatment goals together. "I don't know—you're supposed to tell me," was Denise's automatic reply. Mary carefully made a list of suggested goals, such as increased joint flexibility, lessened pain, enhanced sense of well-being, and feelings of inner calm. "That's fine," Denise agreed.

From then on, the two of them kept track of progress toward the agreed goals and Denise said she enjoyed the sessions. After several months, Denise admitted she did not like feeling responsible for her own care. She liked letting her caregivers tell her what to do, but, of course, if she did not like their approach, she would drop them like a hot potato. She had skipped from one caregiver to another.

This time, Mary insisted on her being part of the planning team, the author of her care, and making conscious choices. Denise started questioning Mary and even disagreed when something did not feel right to her. Mary enjoyed the feistiness that began to emerge and they both started appreciating their relationship. Over time, as the working partnership continued, Denise even agreed to try some of Mary's self-care exercises at home on her own.

Discussion: Therapeutic partnerships are difficult to establish when ingrained beliefs, such as "doctor/caregiver knows all," are present. Passivity is often accompanied by indirect patterns of aggression—a passive-aggressive style that makes sure neither client nor caregiver actually gain much. Mary's perseverance in making goals known and mutually evaluating them paid off in a better and more rewarding relationship than one that might have ended because of Denise's no-one-can-win pattern.

Section IV:

Standards for Creating Healing Relationships with Colleagues, Other Healthcare Professionals, and Our Communities

[T]he world of energy…is a fascinating world, the point of contact for making the unknown, known— and for discovering what we still do not know.
—Cyndi Dale, author

Ethical Principles:

Practitioners of energy therapies treat their colleagues and professionals from other disciplines with respect and honor. They seek to educate other professionals and the public about their special skills, as well as present the theory and research base for their practice.

Related Standards of Practice:

- Energy therapy practitioners (ETPs) refrain from making disparaging remarks concerning other practitioners or professionals. They encourage open exchanges of ideas, and appreciate discussion of theory and research related to energy therapy.

- ETPs discuss personal differences or concerns regarding a colleague's professional conduct directly and privately with the person involved and avoid third-party conversations or triangulation.

- If direct discussion does not bring resolution, ETPs seek arbitration, mediation, or intervention of appropriate organizations, beginning with local resources and moving to regional or national levels as needed.

- ETPs take responsibility for defining and clarifying their practices to local and regional professionals and the public to enhance general awareness in their communities.

- ETPs donate a portion of their time to contribute to general awareness about their profession and to give back to their communities.

CHAPTER TWELVE

BUILDING BRIDGES FOR INNOVATIVE APPROACHES

Although individual practices may seem to be islands of safety away from the concerns of the world, practitioners are connected to the external web of life through their many relationships. These connections include families, friends, referral networks, collegial support groups, consultants with more skill and experience, the natural environment in which we live, and the public whom we serve.

Here we'll consider some of the ways practitioners can establish creative, positive relationships with fellow practitioners and colleagues, interested professionals from other disciplines, and their communities. We'll also look at some of the challenges of introducing innovative methods and their conceptual framework to other professionals and the public. In addition to finding ways to educate others about energy medicine's novel, as-yet experimental approaches, practitioners need to market themselves ethically, learn to handle negativity creatively, and negotiate possible dual relationships and personal vulnerabilities.

One of the challenges of practicing in a new, relatively unknown field is finding ways of communicating effectively regarding concepts that are unfamiliar to most people. Although potential clients will often take a friend's advice to try out a novel method, professionals in most communities are much more likely to be skeptical, sometimes even openly hostile, toward new approaches. Defending one's established turf and beliefs with criticism toward newcomers is a natural response from insiders. It is therefore critical for us as practitioners of energy therapies to communicate effectively about the new orientation we espouse. In addition, demonstrating client-centered values and holding to ethical standards of practice form an essential base for building validity and trust among others in our communities.

My personal outreach experiences have involved teaching Healing Touch for ten years to nurses and allied healthcare personnel all over the United States and then bringing energy psychology concepts to psychotherapists in the past eleven years. There were regional differences in receptivity to energy healing concepts, but, generally, caregivers in institutions that sponsored the programs wanted to learn how they could alleviate pain and emotional distress. Once that intention was clearly understood through weekend workshops, most caregivers embraced the work and began implementing it in their healthcare settings.

Things were quite different in teaching counselors who had individual practices and varying backgrounds. They were oriented to skepticism about novel approaches and had been taught to examine critically theory and research studies of every new modality. Whether they perceived the ideas of energy treatments to be helpful or not, they also evidenced concerns abut how the new paradigm might influence their more conventional practices. They asked many, many questions about standards of care and the ethics of implementing energy modalities. Some considered my stories about positive client outcomes with the methods to be imaginative projections or exaggerations. Fortunately, a fine group of adventuresome psychologists from San Diego persisted over several years and helped me identify and develop more fully some of the needed parameters for individual and group clinical practices. It gave me an opportunity to learn to speak their language and to bring concepts to their world in ways that bridged our various backgrounds.

Possible Theories for
Outcome Mechanisms of Energy Interventions

There is, as yet, no conclusive evidence that gives a single mechanism for the dramatic changes caregivers see in their clients on a daily basis with energy methods, such as pain relief, increased relaxation, reduced anxiety, diminished effects of trauma, enhanced sense of well-being, and the sense of personal empowerment. However, recent scientific research and a number of theories exist that can help answer the most persistently asked question: how do these methods work?

One explanation is to see energy therapy as an extension of the known interaction dynamics of the human mind and body. Thought and imagery have powerful influences on the body's biochemicals, such as endorphin production, via the body's many neurotransmitters into and within cellular structures.[1] As science learns more about these complex interactions, it makes sense that practitioner intention and client goals can bring about powerful effects for increased physical and emotional well-being.

Another viable explanation suggests that a form of reciprocal inhibition is at work when using energy modalities.[2] For example, it is impossible to hold a negative thought or image with its full intensity while at the same time being in the presence of a centered helper who teaches clients how to stimulate specific acupoints, to breathe more deeply, to energize the chakras, or to balance the biofield. It appears from recent research that patterns established within the limbic system of the brain are interrupted when a somatically linked activity of an energy intervention is paired with the memory of a traumatic event.[3] Since repetition of energetic processes through client self-care further enhances release of trauma and anxiety, we may infer that the dual message of the pairing lessens or inhibits the remembrance of affective response. As a result, past events drift safely into the distance as the client begins to live more fully in the present.

The concept of "remembered wellness," from a term coined by Herbert Benson,[4] is another helpful metaphor to explain some of the changes seen with energy treatments. It is well known that the body has a fascinating array of self-healing capacities. Therefore, it's quite likely that the energetic interaction between practitioner and client stimulates the body's own self-regulating mechanisms toward harmony and internal balance. In energetic terms, we describe this by saying that a blocked, congested area of the biofield is modulated or released so that a wholesome flow of *qi* can be restored.

From a psychological perspective, it's also possible that clients access their own deeper potentials through the relaxed peacefulness they feel with energy treatments. Experiencing unconditional caring in a session also engenders a sense of spiritual interconnectedness in many clients.

Cell biologist and biophysicist Dr. James Oschman describes some of the most recent scientific discoveries that lend credibility to the use of energy therapies in *Energy Medicine: The Scientific Basis*. There is not sufficient room to go into all of the fascinating details here, but one example especially caught my imagination. Currently, pulsed electromagnetic field (PEMF) therapy is an accepted device for use in medicine to relieve arthritic pain and joint congestion. It is also effective in jump-starting the healing of wounds and complex bone fractures via its extremely low frequencies that can range from 0.5 to 30 hertz. In a study of the emissions from the hands of experienced Therapeutic Touch practitioners, it was found that centered, experienced caregivers generate very similar electromagnetic pulsations from their hands that cycle within the frequencies of 0.2 to 30 hertz. Intuitively, skilled practitioners can match the recipient's needs in soft or hard tissues by modulating these frequencies.[5] Thus working with an energy practitioner becomes another method for bringing electromagnetic pulsations to clients for relief.

You'll find it helpful to select a theoretical framework that builds bridges to understanding within the concepts known to the listener.

With nurses, I've found mind-body information best in extending the knowledge with which they are familiar; then I can expand to include other theories that give provisional maps of the human vibrational matrix for facilitating physiological and emotional relief. With psychologists, metaphors about the human energy field and its structures are less effective than ideas about reciprocal inhibition, pattern interruption, remembered wellness, and scientific studies. Also, the idea of working to access subconscious potentials, the stored wisdom within clients, resonates well.

We want listeners to understand human energies in a plausible way by extending from the known to the unknown. Reaching out to colleagues, other professionals, and the public requires great flexibility. Capturing the interest of others in terms that can be grasped and at the same time scientifically based is the art. At no time should practitioners make unfounded, exaggerated claims for their modality or give promises that exceed possibility for delivery. Neither should practitioners attempt to mystify their experiences or make the approaches seem obscure or esoteric. Known facts from science, possible theories, interesting metaphors, and case examples—all these go a long way toward establishing healthy rapport with our wider audiences.

Respect Toward Practitioners of Other Disciplines

As mentioned, not all professionals or the public will be receptive to what you know or have to offer. Thus it's vital to keep an open mind toward differing points of view, without any hint of negativity.

Take care to distinguish skeptics from cynics. Skeptics like to ask many questions and seek to find wider frameworks in order to comprehend new information. Cynics are people who reject the validity of anything they do not know or understand. Skeptics want to learn while cynics already have their minds made up and regard new material as untrue. In my years of teaching professionals from every possible discipline, I've found a mix of those patterns as well as people who want to believe almost anything and need to learn to be more discerning. I make it a practice to encourage every question but give cynics a wide berth. I take no responsibility for trying to change their minds. (Cynics seem to derive a kind of internal pleasure from outdoing or defeating the person who tries to get through their walls.)

Every healthcare professional deserves our respect and appreciation for the rich heritage they represent. Often, their profession is also part of the legacy that supports energy healing work. For example, Florence Nightingale had visions of healthcare akin to modern-day integrative health concepts—for healing the body, mind, and spirit of persons and their surroundings. Her insights formed the rubric of modern nursing, the science of statistics, and our current philosophy of human caring so prominent in energy healing.

Today's counselors and healing arts practitioners honor the traditions of Freud's "talking cure," Jung's maps of the unconscious mind, and Maslow's view of all therapies as a means to enhance quality of life for the greater public, not just for those in distress. More recently, Seligman publicized concepts for achieving authentic happiness and influenced current trends toward positive psychology and its emphasis on finding the methods that work best for each individual.[6] This philosophy helped to create an open climate for innovative therapies such as ours to emerge along with complementary approaches to conventional medicine.

Addressing the joint heritage of each professional discipline can be an eloquent and elegant way of reaching practitioners from different disciplines. The goal is always to open doorways to mutual respect. Teaching professional organizations about our innovative work can be very gratifying if we make the effort to understand their frames of reference and historical roots. Authentic willingness to learn from each discipline and its valued standards of care can help us to grow exponentially.

Marketing Your Energy Therapy Practice

Marketing materials—brochures, business cards, promotional items, websites, every e-mail signature, public speaking engagements, or comments in the media—are all a form of contract with the public. Because your marketing efforts are the most visible public representation of your practice, it is extremely important that these communications be factual and educational in nature. If you receive monetary compensation for your work and advertise in any way, you are regarded as a professional practitioner and fall under the laws and statutes established in your region. Therefore, all marketing items should be reviewed with a competent legal professional in your area to make sure they are in compliance with the laws of your locality.

Misrepresentation of one's practice or educational level can create civil or even criminal liabilities, regardless of whether you are licensed or not.[7] For example, clients can sue practitioners for fraud and misleading information if they find the person claims to have expertise in a technique when only minimal training has been received. Certification for a validated program cannot be claimed if it is either in progress or if the certification has lapsed. Thus, caution must be taken if you claim that you are skilled in a modality of which you only have partial knowledge.

State regulatory agencies regularly review marketing materials. Many regulations for healthcare providers are specific about all forms of advertising and how one identifies oneself as a practitioner. Unlicensed providers who advertise services they are not licensed to perform are subject to criminal prosecution. Court cases have tended to interpret state medical practice acts very broadly. A caregiver who is not an MD, for example, is not permitted to give medical advice in any way and could be vulnerable to charges of practicing medicine without a license. Claiming to treat an identified psychiatric diagnosis included in the *DSM-IV* diagnostic manual, such as depression or PTSD, brings a likelihood of being charged with practicing psychotherapy without the required license.

In addition, licensed providers who violate marketing requirements are also subject to professional discipline. Recent examples have occurred in several states where practitioners of energy psychology (a *designated field* that includes specific energy modalities within counseling therapies) have implied that they are psychologists (a *state licensed professional designation*). What you call yourself has to be in line with abilities and credentials.

Care also needs to be taken when a licensed practitioner advertises an innovative technique that is not yet widely accepted. The practitioner's licensing board may consider such methods below the accepted standards for professional practice or outside the scope of practice. In some states, perceived conflicts between the practice of energy therapies and one's licensed profession have been resolved by separating practitioner locales and identifying materials for each activity. Although this may not be ideal, it does provide a temporary solution for resolving possible conflicts until better understandings of integrative practices develop.

Your professional organization is the best ally in supporting the legitimacy of your practice and in helping to resolve conflicts, such as the ones mentioned. (See appendix C for a listing of the most prominent resource organizations for energy professionals.) Openly stating that your methods are novel, innovative, or experimental at this time is honest and in line with integrity.[8] Claims that a method is "proven" or that it can consistently help large populations are not appropriate given the current stage of development in energy practice theory and research.

Sharing case examples for educational purposes must always be done in light of strict confidentiality. Written permission from specific clients is best. Additionally, it's imperative to disguise not only name and facts associated with an example you wish to cite but also any personal information that might be construed to relate to a known individual.

If you think you are an expert in a certain form of energy practice, you need to know that the words "expert" or "specialist" connote ability to give legal testimony. They imply that you know the standard of care in the developing field of energy therapy—something even people with years of experience are loath to do because the field is so new. It's much better to use more general terms to describe yourself, such as someone who "focuses on mind-body integration" or "helps to relieve stress through working with human subtle energies."

Potent practitioners find that focusing on education and sharing with colleagues, other professionals, and the public is much more effective in gaining visibility than glossy marketing brochures or media advertising. Receiving effective referrals and recognition as a professional practitioner is a practical goal. Candid honesty with others about the known and unknown in energy healing engenders trust and respect.

Relating to Colleagues with Different Viewpoints

Since energy modalities are multiplying so rapidly, it's quite likely that several energy practitioners with differing viewpoints, educations, and interests will be in the same community. Some practitioners may have totally different orientations or ways of reaching the public than the paths you value. It can be a challenge to speak truth in a way that avoids judgments or negativity. Bad news always seems to travel much faster than good, so you can be sure that any negative comment about another practitioner, even in a casual conversation, will boomerang in some way. Avoid third-party conversations, anything that resembles gossip, and stay out of the drama triangle.

If you have a concern about another practitioner's actions, seeking direct communication first meets the professional standard. Thinking about ways to do this may challenge you to consider your own shadow material as well as what is troublesome from a more objective perspective. Consultation is a wise way to ensure clarity. Once you're well prepared, speaking with the practitioner in question may even turn into a positive and effective experience.

If conflicting opinions cannot be resolved at the personal level, going to regional or higher levels for remedy is needed. The advantage of being part of a strong professional organization is that many have carefully developed ethical standards of practice and available consultation through ethics committees. Practice dilemmas regarding colleagues in your field should be addressed by appropriately skilled professionals or mediators who can help resolve grievances.

Enhancing Awareness of Energy Practices

Awareness about energy therapies is limited in most areas, so practitioners have excellent opportunities to contribute to education of the public about different energy modalities and their known outcomes. Few professionals from other disciplines know which client issues could best be addressed by a specific energy modality. Helping people in your community identify criteria for selecting a modality or practitioner is a good way to expand visibility without advertising, and speaking about the ethic of caring and the standards you hold builds confidence and respect.

Since most people do not know the standards of which you are aware by reading this book, you could help audiences identify criteria for selection of a practitioner. Here are some sample criteria for prospective clients to consider:

- **Educational level:** What is the educational level of the prospective practitioner, including academic education and time spent in learning the modality?

- **Specific knowledge, experience, and skill:** What are the practitioner's capabilities beyond basic requirements? How many years in practice?

- **Special focus:** What is the practitioner's strongest interest?

- **Willingness to use referral networks and consultation:** Does the practitioner recognize his/her limitations? Is he/she willing to make referrals if complex issues arise?

- **Ethical standards:** Does the practitioner hold a strong ethic of caring? Being client-centered? Willing to listen? Consider options? Keep confidences? Does the person have standards of practice?

- **Personal style:** Is the person compassionate? Does the person "walk his talk" and practice self-care?

- **Results:** What are some of the most likely outcomes of working with the practitioner?

* * * *

The personal and professional style of the practitioner is a strong criterion for selection. Personal humility and willingness to focus on client needs are keys to smooth working relationships. Adhering to identified professional standards builds public confidence in energy practices. Just having a strong educational background and knowledge are not sufficient without the presence of a strong set of ethical principles and professional standards.

CHAPTER THIRTEEN

DEVELOPING THE PROFESSIONAL IMAGE OF ENERGY MODALITIES

The professional image of energy modalities is established and maintained by each of us practitioners. Our commitment to professional standards with their underlying principles of self-regulation is the best way to establish public recognition and acceptance. As appreciation for our methods grows, we will gradually be able to integrate the concepts into mainstream healthcare.

In the meantime, there is much for us to do to spread the word about the value of our interventions and effectiveness in creating a climate of hope, client self-awareness, and insight. Education of the public involves knowing the many practical applications of energy therapies, seeking the mentors we need, developing our referral networks, and dealing with possible vulnerabilities within our profession.

The Value of Energy Interventions

A good place to start developing a vital image for energy medicine practices is to think of the outcomes you've seen and heard about. Personal experiences with clients as well as many vignettes within the growing literature and conferences reiterate the theme of hopefulness that the methods generate. Often, for example, a single session with someone who has been traumatized will reduce the subjective distress clients reported at the outset. Instead of feeling powerless, clients learn tools for self-care that extend beyond the session. Our body-mind work combines positive self-affirmations accompanied by the tapping of selected meridian acupoints, holding specific chakras, balancing the biofield, or using other forms of somatic anchoring. The work can be powerful and fulfilling for both practitioners and clients.

Energy health practitioners are purveyors of hope, especially in situations that cannot be addressed with conventional treatments, such as Western medical practice and cognitive behavioral therapies. For example, recent or past trauma that causes limbic system (midbrain) involvement in the form of flashbacks and nightmares is stored in parts of the brain that form images but are not accessible to verbal, cognitive portions of the brain, such as Broca's region.[1] Attempts at releasing trauma by retelling the story often retraumatizes clients. Until the advent of Eye Movement Desensitization and Reprocessing (EMDR) and energy approaches, used either independently or in combination,[2] there were few effective, rapid ways to relieve the "limbic looping" that causes constant reliving of the trauma.

Another area where energetic approaches offer hope is in providing relief from anxiety. In a nation in which nearly a fifth of the population suffers from some form of anxiety, our interventions and suggestions for client self-care can be lifesaving.[3] Phobias, as a form of specific, often severely handicapping anxiety, can be relieved in minutes rather than the months or years required with more conventional approaches.[4]

Regarding relief of physical symptoms, all forms of energy medicine seem applicable. Long-term physical pain seems to require a whole body-mind approach because medication is seldom sufficient. Well-known research into Therapeutic Touch and Healing Touch supports using energy therapies as an adjunct to conventional medical protocols.[5-8] As clients' thoughts and emotional responses change, they experience a sense of increased self-efficacy and well-being.

Our presentation of the remarkable outcomes we have witnessed and heard about must always be factual and exact, hence my dedication to including in this book references with which you may already be familiar. The best way for us as practitioners to spread the good news about energy therapies is to offer clear, professionally acknowledged backup information for our work.

Many practitioners have developed their own one-page information sheet, written in layperson's terms, about the specific therapy they offer. Sample titles include "Emotional acupressure to relieve distress" and "Energy medicine first aid for physical needs."

Because there is an avalanche of information about energy medicine that is sensationalized and lacking full comprehension, laypersons often make assumptions that are half-truths or outright errors. To illustrate, one client asked her practitioner recently, "Do you believe the mind can prevent and remove disease?" In truth, the answer would be both yes and no. We've learned the mind is a powerful ally in healing, that the human energy system appears to be designed to self-regulate and restore wellness, and that effective imagery and mind-body interventions can release energy blockages and promote health. However, there are thousands of unknown factors in the causation and presence of illness, including environmental toxins, each person's unique responses to various stressors, chemical imbalances, familial patterns, and genetic predispositions.

It's both presumptuous and dangerous to claim that energetic interventions, imagery, or affirmations can prevent or cure illness. What we can acknowledge is that we help to create a climate, a healing environment, in which the whole person's curative mechanisms may come into action. Some people's bodies may be too weakened to improve, but their emotional, mental, and spiritual issues can resolve and provide alternate forms of healing. Other clients may have breakthroughs that allow total remission of their physical symptoms, but they leave treatment without gaining any particular psychological insights. How and how much change happens appears to be a very individual process.

Our professional standard is to foster the sacred space for hope. One or more aspects of our clients' energy systems can always improve, even in the face of physical aging, family upheavals, or the dying process.

Selecting Consultants or Mentors

I highly recommend that practitioners, especially those who are new to the field, enlist the help of a consultant or mentor in establishing the professional image of their practice. While a consultant may have advanced expertise in your field and is compensated accordingly, a mentor may be a trusted friend or colleague with whom you exchange ideas and generate plans of action.

Similar to the criteria given for helping prospective clients to select a practitioner, selecting a mentor or consultant needs to be based on objective as well as subjective evaluation. In many well-established energy modalities, such as Healing Touch, mentoring by advanced certified practitioners is required to develop a caregiving practice. Fortunately, there is a strong tradition of generosity among those practitioners, which includes their willingness to share knowledge and talents.

Criteria for selection of a consultant include finding a practitioner who holds a strong knowledge base from academic learning and the curriculum of the modality you know as well as demonstrated skills in good communications and a period of time in successful practice. Strong recommendations from others who have experienced the individual's coaching are usually indicative of competence. Your intuitive sense of a match with such a practitioner will help your personal awareness to grow. A good mentor will also help you define your strengths and weaknesses and encourage your development as an effective caregiver.

The willingness and wisdom to seek consultation for complex client issues or dilemmas is the hallmark of a professional caregiver. Friends are likely to agree with you, but a remunerated professional whom you do not know is much more likely to provide the sound advice you need to avoid disservice to clients or possible legal entanglement.

Selecting Your Sources for Giving and Receiving Referrals

Energy healing practitioners need to establish good solid referral networks to navigate the complex needs of clients. Establishing referral networks also helps you be known by professionals who would refer some of their clients to you. The two-way street of referral networking requires attentive nurturing. If you are a newcomer to your community, you would do well to meet with established practitioners both in specialty areas and general conventional practices. While friends and colleagues can provide support and information, reaching out to other disciplines takes focused intention.

One way to reach allied healthcare professionals is to offer training in the philosophy, theory, and research that supports your energy therapy modality. Demonstrating a selected method for group learning is another elegant way to increase helpful connections. Personally seeking selected practitioners to experience their care is the best way to know what your clients might receive. For example, if you're a counselor, you need to know somatic therapists and massage practitioners who can address the tension held in clients' bodily structures. By learning from your own contacts, you will know which therapists to recommend to clients. Similarly, if you are a massage professional, as many energy practitioners are, you will want to know counselors or psychologists who can assist your clients in releasing deeply held trauma that is beyond your scope of practice.

The suggestion to learn from personally experiencing another professional's care may seem expensive in time and cost. However, it's a worthy investment for opening a practice and becoming known. The possibility of doing exchanges with selected practitioners also exists and brings with it the opportunity of letting other professionals know about your approaches and skills.

Referral networks should include a variety of skilled professionals you have come to trust. Here is a listing of essential disciplines within which to network in order to address client needs that exceed your scope of practice:

- Counseling specialties—marriage, family, child, individual, group practitioners.

- Chiropractic arts to deal with structural body issues.

- Psychiatry—especially for medication evaluation or medical supervision of clients.

- General medicine practice—for medical evaluation and ongoing physical monitoring.

- Massage therapists and other forms of body-oriented work.

- Practitioners who are skilled in dealing with various forms of nonordinary states of consciousness.

- Social workers—for agency contacts, placement needs, and financial consultation.

- Spiritual consultants either from the client's religious affiliation or from a person who is acceptable to the client's belief system.

As can be seen, an integrative approach to care for the whole person requires knowing and using a large number of resources. Energy interventions are holistic, integrative by their very nature. No practitioner should expect to address all aspects needed for multidimensional healing. Our standard of care is to work respectfully with those whose talents can help bring about the best possible client outcomes.

Professional Vulnerabilities Related to Referrals

Legal Liabilities

Energy practitioners who do not make needed referrals may actually face legal liability for negligence. Ordinarily, energy practitioners have no malpractice liability when referring a client to a known and appropriately credentialed healthcare practitioner. There are exceptions, however.[9] For one, there is the legal concept of "direct liability," which is an area of concern if your referral practitioner shows lack of due care that results in some form of client injury. Another legal theory operating in relation to referrals is "vicarious liability." If the referring caregiver sends a client to a provider who is known to be incompetent, the referring person is liable.

Another aspect is the liability of aiding or abetting a crime if a referral results in grievous bodily injury or death of a client. This may occur in two ways: (1) when the practitioner refers the patient to an unlicensed practitioner, such as a homeopath or another energy healer who is deemed to be practicing medicine or psychology without a license; and (2) when referral is made to a licensed provider, such as an acupuncturist or chiropractor, who exceeds the legally authorized scope of his designated practice.

Knowing these risks will help you make carefully considered referrals, but that does not mean you cannot refer to unlicensed providers. As long as unlicensed providers do not make promises of curing and do not claim to be a substitute for biomedical or psychological assessment, they are not subject to prosecution under medical practice acts.

Addressing Client Feelings about a Referral

People in need are often quite pleased to have a bond with energy practitioners. They may not fully understand the wisdom of your wishing to make a referral. Maintaining rapport with clients so they do not feel abandoned by your suggestion is vital. Often, specialty professionals give their treatments for a brief time so clients return to you when they have completed; at other times, clients can continue to experience support from you during the time they're also receiving specialty treatment.

Clients return from the referral source with added wisdom and insight. They often come to see the referring practitioner as their central advocate for well-being. Like many practitioners, my clients have come to value my referrals and appreciate my willingness to help them reach

their goals. I have never lost a relationship with a client because of referring, but I have had some regrets about not using my referral network
soon enough. Remember that clients' appreciation and word-of-mouth
communication are your best forms of marketing and, rest assured, your
integrity in making appropriate referrals will be rewarded.

Avoiding Dual Relationships

A dual relationship is possible any time you as a practitioner are
involved with a client beyond the parameters of the sacred contract the
two of you have set. Dual relationships occur in the simple act of treating someone who is already known to you, such as a friend or family
member. Complex interactions are difficult to avoid in smaller communities and require attention to set boundaries that are acceptable to both
parties and include strict confidentiality. For example, you may choose
to treat a friend several times during a crisis but not charge. Or you may
find it's too challenging to keep the different roles separate and refer to
another practitioner, which may include telephone consultation from a
different location.

Dual relationships also include the more obvious overlap that happens when there are conflicts of interest. For example, recommending or
selling a vitamin, product, or device when you are the treating professional constitutes a direct conflict of interest: you function as a salesper-
son and as the empowered caregiver. The power differential is very much
at work in making sales or in giving concrete advice to clients; they are
likely to acquiesce but possibly have later regrets. If a practitioner seeks
financial advice from a client who is a stockbroker, the client functions
as both client and helper. If you ask a client to attend a play or performance in which you are involved, you are both therapist and performer,
creating role confusion.

The power differential usually makes clients willing to follow suggestions. When clients come to believe at a later time that the fiduciary
relationship of trust was harmed, practitioner vulnerabilities proliferate.
Numerous lawsuits have been opened by former clients who, after treat-

ment ended, came to think differently about the care they received. The best way to prevent unfavorable hindsight is to provide frequent openings for clients to express their concerns during the course of treatment. The standard of care is to take responsibility for being proactive to prevent any action that could be deemed a conflict of interest.

It has been a joy for me to offer energy interventions (usually of the general biofield balancing or pain-relieving variety) to family members. Yet, while some family members have responded with delight and enthusiasm, others have been skeptical or negative. Family expectations are especially likely to present complex relationship issues for professional practitioners. No practitioner should assume that there is an agreement to use energy methods with family members unless the practitioner has clear informed consent, coupled with respect for the relative's choices. In close relationships, it is true that one's explanations of the work may be briefer and confirmation may come in the form of a nod rather than a signed document, but assent needs to be clearly given nonetheless. Hesitancy or doubt on the part of the prospective recipient are cues to wait for another time. Taking any response personally is detrimental to ongoing relationships. Never assume anything about people you think you know!

Dual relationships with friends and family members can be addressed by staying within the professional standard that says, "Offer what you can appropriately give and let the other person decide." The clear power differential with our children suggests that we tread very lightly and with humor in suggesting a self-care method. If they accept, it's to their benefit that we've explored the new territories of energy healing.

Working in Group and Public Settings

Principles of energy therapies are not limited to one-on-one private care settings. Many practitioners have found receptive audiences among businesspeople, computer technologists, schoolteachers, and performing artists, all of whom were looking for effective ways to help themselves. In school settings, biofield balancing methods such as those included in Brain Gym[10] are a fine way to teach children self-management. Also, energy balancing is helpful to parent and teacher groups. Some practitioners have columns in newspapers or public listings about classes. Energetic applications in the business world include teaching stress management skills for all levels within an organization. Using energy methods with established, ongoing groups and work settings, of course, requires group agreement to informed consent and confidentiality.

* * * *

In the present time of increasing environmental concerns, energy practitioners would do well to understand that our energies are inextricably intertwined with the natural world. We can tap into the unlimited supply of energy that exists for the planet within the solar system. Everyone on "spaceship earth" needs the centered presence that we've learned about to steer a steady course in troubled waters. I have personally worked with several environmental groups to help them center and hold their focus in the face of intense social and political challenges. We all so need the peacefulness of a large old-growth forest in order to realign with the harmony of nature that nurtures, supports, and refocuses us!

VIGNETTES FOR SECTION IV

Vignette IV.1 Hearing Bad News about Another Practitioner

Don asks his personal friend, energy practitioner Steve, "What do you think of Dr. K.?" As Steve questions him further, he finds out that Dr. K. is a psychiatrist who did several energy practices with Don. In a subsequent session, Dr. K. scolded Don for not doing the methods correctly. Now that he's talking with Steve, Don states that Dr. K. is not very compassionate. What's more, Dr. K. spoke publically about a clinically relevant part of Don's life without his permission.

Steve was temped to say, "I told you so," because Don chose Dr. K. against Steve's advice. But he resisted the urge and thought of the professional standard for encouraging Don, the client, to speak to Dr. K., his practitioner, about his complaints and feelings. If Steve were to get involved immediately, the possibility of triangulation becomes very real. Steve also recognizes that many clients are unwilling to speak up because of the power differential. So Steve helped Don explore feelings about speaking with integrity to his provider. What other actions might you consider to help in the situation?

Discussion: If Steve felt that Dr. K.'s behavior was damaging to the professional image of energy therapy, he would be correct in attempting to speak directly with Dr. K. as a fellow practitioner while keeping Don's name confidential. The art would be to do this in a way that helped Dr. K. increase his awareness and learn to respect the practice of energy modalities more assiduously. Steve could also report the behavior to Dr. K.'s professional organization, knowing that their first step would likewise be to encourage direct communication with the client in question, long before considering any disciplinary action.

Think of handling similar practitioner complaint situations in tiers—the first and best is to foster direct communication between clients and their providers of care and to educate clients on how remaining silent perpetuates the problem. If direct communication is not possible even with your support, then you might attempt direct communication with the other professional, either by yourself or with a third person to mediate, and document the visit. Finally, communication via the professional association is another option, a necessary one in some circumstances.

Each step has challenges and rewards. In the case of a silent, unwilling client, direct discussion with the practitioner in question can be effective because all professionals want to be well regarded. If the professional organization becomes involved, the issues are usually resolved informally as well. Since energy therapy is such a new field, classic cases and precedent-setting decisions have not yet been documented. Each practitioner has to learn to take responsibility for defining the standard for acceptable, appropriate behavior and communicating clearly with other professionals.

Vignette IV.2 Finding a Good Practitioner

Mrs. Smith asks you at a workshop to tell her who is a good practitioner in the field of energy therapy. This is a great opportunity to educate her about selecting a practitioner in line with the important criteria identified in chapter 12. You may also help her to know you and your standards, which could help her to consider seeking your services.

You may begin by listing the skills required to be an energy healing caregiver. Beyond educational classes, there is learning via mentorship with other practitioners and compilation of case management materials. Every professional caregiver should be willing to share his or her background and learning pathways.

You could also talk about the personal qualities that Mrs. Smith might value in a practitioner. Attention to ethics and professional standards should be evident in the person's marketing materials and in discussions. Encouraging someone like Mrs. Smith to interview several practitioners is also a good strategy, since that will empower her to make the best decision for herself. Not many people buy the first car they see on a lot. We should encourage people who ask us for recommendations to be equally, if not more, discriminating when selecting a caregiver who will interact with their energy field, influencing both health and wellness.

You could also encourage Mrs. Smith to think of specific questions she would like to ask potential practitioners, such as: What is your experience in working with the kind of symptoms I have? Have you had results in dealing with anxiety attacks? Would you be willing to refer me if my needs exceeded your level of practice?

In other words, you could make the discussion with Mrs. Smith educational by encouraging her to see broader perspectives and helping her identify specific needs and preferences.

Vignette IV.3 Helping an Indecisive Client

Dana was a social worker who met an elderly client named Emily who was under a great deal of stress. As they worked together, it became apparent that Emily was under the negative influence of her adult daughter and the daughter's boyfriend—both of whom she considered to be her "only children." In the previous year, the pair had persuaded Emily to sell her large home in an affluent neighborhood, give them the proceeds so they could buy rental properties for their gain, and move in with them in another state. Emily did not adjust easily to her new one-room setting and became clinically depressed, especially since her "children" were not interested in helping her find social contacts. Whenever Emily thought of returning to the state where she had friends, they told her that there was no money for a trip and she should forget her friends. She became a prisoner of their greed and demands.

Dana began to realize the possibility of fiscal and emotional elder abuse in the situation. She contacted fellow professionals in a nearby city and state board to find out which behaviors of "the children" were in the line of abuse and required reporting. Since the abuse was too subtle to meet the criteria for mandatory reporting in that state, Dana contacted the state senior services to find out what could be done to help Emily. It turned out that Emily was considered a "willing victim" in the situation and functioned as someone too weak to make up her mind to find relief. Emily was unwilling to let Dana file a complaint, so they had to wait until Emily was willing to take action. In the meantime, Dana did all she could to keep Emily aware of the issues and her rights to explore further options for her life. Dana also established a good referral relationship with a local senior services caseworker who was able to get financial details in case further action was requested. Together Dana and the caseworker stayed in touch with Emily over many months.

The case blew open when "the children" tried to have Emily declared legally incompetent because of her age and to obtain conservatorship for her. Because the helpful relationship had been established, Dana and her resources were able to help Emily get some of her money back and to move to a more congenial environment of her choice.

The events of this case took well over a year. Dana was puzzled because she was facing factors that were unfamiliar to her and exacerbated by her client's ambivalence. If it were not for the professional networks available by telephone, Internet, and consultation, Dana could not have met the ethical standard of working to find what would best serve her client.

Vignette IV.4 Dual Relationship: Renter and Provider of Care

Lovebirds Jenny and Ian came for relationship consultation with Dr. Jane after three months of living together. Jane taught them ways of defusing some of the intense arguments they had by balancing their biofield energies, tapping acupoints when they triggered each other, and refocusing on the intention of their relationship. They did quite well over six sessions until Ian declared that Dr. Jane should pay him.

It turned out that Jenny was the office manager of the large building Jane used for her practice and that Ian owned the facility. Since Jane was paying a fixed rental fee, Ian felt that part of the fee she was charging the couple should be returned to him and Jenny. There was nothing Jenny or Jane could do to convince him that the fee paid for services to a counselor is different from the rent paid to an owner of a building.

After seeking consultation from another therapist, Jane was able to find a different office in which to see the couple from then on. She returned the money Ian felt was his to remove any impediments to the successful interventions they had been receiving. Her priority throughout was to help the couple.

As time went on, Jenny began to see other areas in which Ian was irrational, greedy, and stubborn. Jenny continued therapy, but Ian dropped out and the couple separated within a year.

Discussion: At the time they met, Jane was only vaguely aware that Jenny was the office manager for Ian's enterprise. As soon as she found out about the dual relationship, which could have occurred with the intake session, she would have been better off to refer the couple to another therapist to prevent complications.

Vignette IV.5 Potential Dual Relationship: Writer's Group

Carol was an energy therapist who lived in a small town. A friend organized a writer's group based on a self-help book for authors. As people signed up for the ongoing group, Carol learned that three of her strongest clients had also joined the group.

Carol wondered if this would be a conflict of interest, since writer's groups tend to share intimate details of their lives. She asked a colleague in another community as well as a professional within her national professional organization. Both agreed that there was the potential of a dual relationship unless each client honestly felt positive about Carol's presence and the bond of confidentiality they had made with her. Carol then wondered if she would feel comfortable sharing details of her personal life in front of them.

When Carol asked each of the clients their feelings about her presence, they seemed surprised that she would ask. However, they also stated how honored they felt by her willingness to ask. With full consent from each individual, Carol attended the writer's group. After several meetings, though, Carol decided the group was not the kind of support she needed for herself as a professional and joined a group in another county where she was unknown.

Discussion: This is an interesting example of how professionals can be proactive in preventing possible conflicts of interest. Checking with colleagues and professional associations can be very helpful, but the subtleties of group interactions can often not be known ahead of time. In the end, the caregiver's assessment of her personal needs for more support won out.

Vignette IV.6 Handling a Client's Secret

A client you have been working with reveals that he often thinks of ending his life but does not want anyone, especially his family, to know. He states that he trusts you with the information because you are his only friend and will understand his need for secrecy. He has a plan and will use it when he feels he cannot go on.

It is your professional responsibility to warn at least one significant other in the client's life. How can you let the client know without alienating him that it is your duty to breach confidentiality if someone makes threats of harm to self or others? What alternatives might you help the client consider? What resources could you draw on to find the best solutions?

This example is very real and could create practitioner stress. Ideally, because of the ethical standards around informed consent, the client would already know that practitioners have a duty to break confidences to appropriate resources if a client intends to harm self or others. Many members of the lay public are also aware of this standard of care, so it's quite likely that the client in the situation is exploring the practitioner's response and asking for help indirectly rather than making a conclusive decision.

In similar situations, I've spent time with suicidal ideation clients to find out what is causing their despair and to let our work together begin movement toward healing of the intense pain that must be present. I also try to find out which significant other they would be willing for me to contact or with whom they would be willing to participate in a three-way conversation. Experienced consultation for the caregiver is always a good idea along with possible referrals for social services and/or medical evaluation to ease the client's depression.

* * * *

As we can see in these vignettes, community resources are important allies in our work. Each scenario has its own twists and turns, and there are often no straightforward answers. Rather, we hold a steady compass by paying careful attention to our uneasiness about a situation and then try to find the best solutions in partnership with the client and the resources of wider community contacts.

CHAPTER FOURTEEN

FUTURE DEVELOPMENTS AS
ENERGY THERAPIES MATURE

All truth goes through three stages—first it is ridiculed, then it is violently opposed, and finally it is accepted as being self-evident.
—Arthur Schopenhauer, philosopher

E nergy therapy practices are based on the core values of heart-centered human caring to meet client needs directly. We've explored the practice of energy therapies by looking at the broad ethical principles and the related standards for professional action that flow from those principles. In this book, creating a healthy ethic of caring has focused on looking at the creation of healthy, appropriate relationships. These respectful, caring relationships can develop when each practitioner takes responsibility for:

- Being aware of and in harmony with self.

- Being sensitive in each interaction with clients.

- Being alert and receptive to local and wider communities.

- Being in step with laws and regulations that cover every professional practitioner, whether licensed or unlicensed.

The most currently pertinent standards related to each of the four areas have been listed at the beginning of each section and then discussed and explored in more depth in chapters 3 through 13. These standards become the yardstick, or professional benchmark, for you to measure and maximize your effectiveness with clients and your community while at the same time attending to your personal safety and providing necessary risk management.

To summarize our discussion, here are some questions to ask yourself regarding each of the four principles that are the focus of this book.

Exercise 14.1 Checklist for Establishing Healthy Relationships in Your Energy Practice

- **Regarding legal aspects of conducting a practice:** Am I aware of the legal requirements for conducting a practice open to the public in my region, district, county, or incorporated city? Are my marketing materials in line with legally correct concepts and terminology? Am I performing services and giving attention to items in a manner similar to anyone in a similar situation? Am I doing anything that could be potentially harmful to my client (possible breaches that could be considered *malpractice*)? Am I omitting anything that should be considered for optimal client care (possible breaches that could be considered *negligence*)?

- **Regarding personal awareness of yourself as a practitioner:** Am I harboring any feelings of uneasiness or distress that I should explore more fully? Am I aware of my chakra vulnerabilities in relation to specific clients and other professionals? Am I actively engaging in risk management practices? Am I aware of my limitations regarding specific client issues? Do I refer as needed? Do I seek consultation to resolve areas of uneasiness? Am I appropriately honoring and nurturing my intuitional and spiritual gifts?

- **Regarding your relationship with each client:** Do I have clear informed consent that includes statements of benefits, risks, and client choice? Is my client really my priority? Do I monitor client responses before, during, and after each intervention? Do I ask clients for feedback about a session or feelings about our relationship to prevent any later regrets or backlash? Do I stay within the boundaries set in my agreements with clients? If change to an agreement is needed, do I discuss changes for mutual consideration? Am I aware of the four main survival archetypes operating within myself and my clients? Am I aware of archetypal patterns that may emerge in each client relationship?

- **Regarding your relationship to fellow practitioners, other professionals, and your community:** Do I seek healthy interactions with fellow practitioners? Do I share my knowledge and skills with other professionals? Do I frame public presentations to fit the audience and their interests? Is my list of referral sources current and sufficient for a wide variety of client needs? Are my marketing materials accurate and frequently updated? Am I willing to take responsibility for ensuring that ethical standards are upheld by fellow energy care practitioners? Do I know which channels to follow for registering my concerns?

There is much to consider, but the bottom line is holding onto your good sense, knowing and trusting your inner wisdom, and being closely in tune with the client as healing partner. Never go it alone! Always know that there are ample resources for help in the form of mentors, consultants, professional networks, and organizations.

It is up to us to determine future directions for our field, which is growing and maturing in both wisdom and strength. As the practice of energy therapy continues to mature in the coming years, we can even now envision some of the most likely developments. With a cautionary crystal ball and a big dose of intuition, I believe we'll see emergence of the following broad directions:

- There will be a steady increase in public acceptance of energy modalities.
- Our discipline will establish criteria for evaluating new modalities in energy therapy.
- Ethical principles and standards will come to be seen as the leading edge of our discipline.

- Energy therapies will be perceived as the beacon of hope in a rapidly changing world and global uncertainty.

Increase in Public Acceptance of Energy Therapies

All of us who are involved with energy approaches see a bright future for increased public acceptance. It's quite likely that noninvasive energetic modalities will take their place as a form of "first aid" for most stress-elated issues and will be sought and tried before using more complex and invasive methods, such as medication or surgical interventions. Application of our work will likely increase in all walks of life—businesses, schools, homes, community groups[1]—and energy therapists with many backgrounds will include counselors, life coaches, educators, artists, clergy, human resources personnel, friends, and neighbors who care about each other.

Leading energy psychology and energy medicine theorist David Feinstein envisions that ongoing scientific and evidential studies will demonstrate that the methods "provide neurologically potent interventions for strengthening the mental habits and attitudes that promote …well-being." As evidence of effectiveness mounts, Dr. Feinstein envisions that increasing numbers of people, both lay and professional, will explore energy interventions and cause the field to "refine the procedures, demonstrate the necessary and sufficient conditions for effective intervention, and identify the powers and limitations of the approach(es)."[2] Energy treatments will be relevant not only for relief of physical distress, but will also be increasingly accepted as a vehicle for enhancing emotional intelligence, optimism, positive self-affirmation, and self-esteem.

As suggested in the quote from Schopenhauer, it's also quite likely that some forms of backlash will increase. Pharmaceutical corporations may feel threatened by the explosion of effective self-help methods that will decrease public need for mood-altering medications, tranquilizers, or pain formulations. In addition, traditional psychotherapies have much invested in certain styles of long-term treatment. As research validates the efficacy of energy therapy approaches, insurance companies, who have little investment in particular ideologies except for their own goals for profit, may come to recognize that energy medicine is more rapid, efficient, and cost-effective than conventional care and begin to require early exploration with energy approaches. Ridicule about our unusual or "weird-looking" methodologies may change to forms of open opposition before energy medicine becomes accepted as a self-evident truth.

Most certainly, concerns over ethics, standards, and legal aspects will emerge as our practices develop and reach greater numbers of people. The likelihood of touching into issues not yet anticipated or known is quite real given the complexity of each human situation. Some groups will also question training and competence of practitioners, scope of practice parameters, and possible misuse of the processes for one's personal gain or manipulation of the public.

The concerns I've attempted to address in this book are a beginning step toward the careful considerations that each practitioner and related professional organizations must make. It is my hope that the awareness created by this discussion will continue to increase and expand as our discipline develops to its full and useful potentials for giving care within mainstream healthcare.

Definition of Criteria for Evaluating New Modalities

What's true and accepted in the present is clearly not the last word about our field. Since the first use of energy methods in the early 1970s, our field has grown rapidly in both depth and breadth. We recall that there are currently more than 250 energy-related modalities in use in the United States.[3] New modalities are likely to emerge with the synergy of creative minds so evident at national and international conferences, while modalities focused primarily on a single leader or an ad hoc issue may fall into disuse. Consolidation or mergers to increase visibility and recognition may also be seen in the future.

Another growing trend is for universities and external degree programs for advanced education to integrate established energy modalities into their educational curriculums as the Academy of Intuition Medicine has done with its graduate programs in the San Francisco area. Current examples found in places of higher learning are the standardized certification programs offered by the Association for Comprehensive Energy Psychology (ACEP), Therapeutic Touch (TT), and the Healing Touch Program (HTP) (contact information in appendix C). Ongoing updates within each specialty and continuing education will be needed to keep pace with new advances.

As new methods develop, the community of energy practitioners needs to be willing to evaluate them for validity and effectiveness. Criteria for evaluation need to be clear and facilitate access to information for the public. So far the bottom lines for evaluation have been: Is it effective? Is it safe? What is the cost-to-benefit ratio? More sophisticated means to judge new, innovative approaches that will emerge have to be developed if practitioners are going to address the needs of the public and at the same time continue to honor the already standing work of committed, ethical facilitators.

Commitment to ethical principles and professional standards mandates a spirit of openness toward new modalities along with a willingness to hold to the values that have already been established. Based on standards and criteria considered in section IV, current practitioners can help the public to differentiate the more consistently useful modalities from those that are less effective, have less scientific backing, or make exorbitant claims.

Ethics and Professional Standards Constitute the Leading Edge of Our Endeavors

Clearly, the delivery of caring practices lies at the dynamic, evolving edge of our discipline. Professional standards—radiating from our central values and flowing from our relationship to ourselves, to our clients, to our community, and to relevant legal aspects—are the essence of the caregiver's intention put into action. It matters very much how we handle minor breaches related to our chakra vulnerabilities, how we seek consultation and use referral sources, how we assist and support new practitioners, how we communicate to the public, how we bring caring consciousness into every interaction, and how we honor and respect ourselves. Paying attention to these considerations is the hallmark of a professional field that is growing and healthy. Practitioners who pretend they are not at risk, unfortunately, open the door to creating a negative image for the profession, to legal consequences, and, eventually, to undesirable regulatory actions.

As visibility for energy therapies grows, it's quite likely that the National Institutes of Health or other publicly controlled agency involved with energy medicine within complementary approaches will require practitioners to definitively establish and maintain professional standards along with mandating stricter educational credentials. Having thinking and action along these lines already in place will significantly validate and support wise practitioners.

Many leading organizations for energy practitioners already require specific foundational courses before a person can take training in their modality. They also mandate supervisory time and comprehension of professional standards derived from their codes of ethics before recognizing and certifying their practitioners. New programs, for example, are expanding their criteria for laypersons to become recognized as an entry-level student. Laypersons without a social sciences background are increasingly required to demonstrate competencies in handling client dilemmas either by taking courses or demonstrating proficiency to identified standards, such as the ones named in this book.

Energy therapy practitioners are also increasingly eligible for and carrying malpractice insurance, which is evidence of their professionalism. Although few programs require it, it is always a good idea to protect yourself with some known financial backup in case of client dissatisfaction. Healing Touch leads the way by offering a low-cost program of malpractice insurance for its practitioners as well as for unlicensed caregivers from a large number of related energy therapy practices.[4]

Every one of us who practices an energy modality will have opportunity to demonstrate the valid and growing interest in ethical, professional standards of care. We are creating the foundation for the future by ensuring positive perceptions in our relationships with clients and our communities. We are privileged to have the opportunity at this time: we are mandated to do our best with knowledge, skill, and self-insight.

Energy Therapies
as a Beacon in Times of Major Global Change

The present global situation of rapid change and uncertainty underscores the need for centered and focused innovators to lead the way by holding themselves steady in the midst of storms. Although the pain of our changing world and environment may not always be evident, it is an ever-present background as we consider healing for ourselves and for others. Nations worldwide are in the midst of a major shift in human consciousness, one much greater and further reaching than the previous agricultural and industrial revolutions. Humanity is at a major turning point, "The Great Turning" as futurist Joanna Macy[5] calls it. It is the shift from the self-limiting behaviors of corporate powers to finding viable paths for a sustainable future. It is a painful time, as political powers wrestle with the questions that impact not just quality of life, but also our very existence on the planet. One truth is certain from our understanding of energy therapies—we are interconnected with each other as never before. Our interrelationships are inextricably woven into the web of life and all other living beings. What affects one of us, affects everyone.

Energy modalities offer hope in this somewhat gloomy scenario. Human beings carry within their own energy systems the very resources that remind them who they really are: energy beings having a temporary human experience. With this in mind, dedicated caregivers can hold their steady light and offer their compassion to others. Our ethic of compassion is demonstrated not only by avoiding activity that may cause harm, but also by consciously seeking and developing generous, positive qualities within ourselves. It takes conscious and deliberate intention to cultivate positive habits. Inner dispositions change when a person commits to engaging patience, tolerance, forgiveness, respect, and willingness to learn. With such resources, human ideals and values come alive as engines of progress.

The Dalai Lama writes, "Genuine happiness is characterized by inner peace and arises in the context of our relationships with others. It therefore depends on ethical conduct. This in turn consists in acts which take others' well-being into account."[6] An ethic of human caring is not only needed—it can transform our world from its infatuation with the love of power to the power of love, from living by the Rule of Gold to living by the Golden Rule as taught in Christianity and other faiths.

All human beings seek to be happy and avoid suffering: our differences really are minimal when compared to the shared goals of honoring the web of life on this planet. If we are in harmony with ourselves and our values, our relationships with others will have integrity. If we are incoherent, unable to define our purpose and intention, our relationships will also be distorted.

It is my hope that reading this book has increased your esteem for your gifts as well as broadened your view of energy therapy practice. Having explored these considerations in more depth will undoubtedly increase your ability to function fully and joyously as an effective practitioner.

In using the concepts and resources suggested here, may you find courage in the spirit of a blessing from poet John O'Donohue:

A new confidence will come alive

To urge you toward higher ground

Where your imagination

Will learn to engage difficulty

As its most rewarding threshold.[7]

Appendix A

Further
Recommended Reading

Ethical Standards of Caring for Our Time

Barstow, C. (2006) *Right Use of Power: The heart of ethics.* Boulder, CO: Many Realms Publishing.

Cohen, M. H. (2003) *Future Medicine: Ethical dilemmas, regulatory challenges, and therapeutic pathways to health care and healing in human transformation.* Ann Arbor, MI: University of Michigan Press.

The Dalai Lama, (1999) *Ethics for a New Millennium.* New York: Riverhead Books.

Feinstein, D. (2011) *Ethics Handbook for Energy Healing Practitioners.* Santa Rosa, CA: Energy Psychology Press.

Myss, C. (2001) *The Sacred Contract: Awakening your divine potential.* New York: Harmony Books.

Plante, T. G. (2004) *Do the Right Thing: Living ethically in an unethical world.* Oakland, CA: New Harbinger Publications.

Taylor, K. (1995) *The Ethics of Caring: Honoring the web of life in our professional healing relationships.* Santa Cruz, CA: Hanford Mead.

Publications Related to Current Energy Modalities

Bengston, W. (2010) *Chasing the Cure: An effective alternative for treating cancer and other diseases.* Toronto, Ontario: Key Porter Books.

Church, D. (2007) *The Genie in Your Genes: Epigenetic medicine and the new biology of intention.* Santa Rosa, CA: Energy Psychology Press.

Dale, C. (2010) *The Subtle Body: An encyclopedia of your energetic anatomy.* Boulder, CO: Sounds True.

Doidge, N. (2007) *The Brain that Changes Itself: Stories of personal triumph from the frontiers of brain science.* New York: Penguin Books.

Eden, D. (1998) *Energy Medicine: Balance your body's energies for optimum health, joy, and vitality.* New York: Jeremy Tarcher/Putnam.

Gruder, D. (2008) *The New IQ: How integrity intelligence serves you, your relationships, and our world.* Santa Rosa, CA: Elite Books.

Hover-Kramer, D. (2009) *Healing Touch Guidebook: Practicing the art and science of human caring.* San Antonio, TX: Healing Touch Program Press.

Hover-Kramer, D. (2009) *Second Chance at Your Dream: Engaging your body's energy resources for optimal aging, creativity, and health.* Santa Rosa, CA: Energy Psychology Press.

Judith, A. (2006) *Waking the Global Heart: Humanity's rite of passage from the love of power to the power of love.* Santa Rosa, CA: Elite Books.

O'Donohue, J. (2008) *To Bless the Space Between Us.* New York: Doubleday.

Oschman, J. L. (2002) *Energy Medicine: The scientific basis.* Edinburgh, UK: Churchill Livingstone/Harcourt.

Thomas, L. (2010) *The Encyclopedia of Energy Medicine.* Minneapolis, MN: Fairview Press.

Watson, J. (2008) *Nursing: The philosophy and science of caring.* Boulder, CO: University of Colorado Press.

Appendix B

Sample Forms

Disclaimer

This information is provided only as a general recommendation. It is not intended to give legal advice or be a substitute for the necessary step of obtaining legal counsel from a licensed attorney in your region, county, or municipality who knows its legal parameters for practice.

If you are a licensed professional, it is also necessary to determine if you are within the scope of practice of your profession in using energy modalities.

Readers should not act upon this information without having professional legal counsel.

I. Sample Informed Consent
for Treatment with an Energy Therapy Approach

I have been informed about the new field of therapeutic practice that works with one or more aspects of the human energy system to bring about body-mind relief. In addition, I have been informed about scientific studies that are confirming the value of these approaches for releasing trauma and anxiety as well as increasing relaxation, reducing pain sensation, and enhancing a sense of well-being. I have been advised that there are currently no known side effects or detrimental results when energy-oriented treatments are properly administered by a qualified, experienced practitioner.

I further understand that, because these methods are relatively new, the extent and breadth of their effectiveness, including benefits and risks, are not yet fully known. I have been advised of the following:

- Vivid or traumatic memories may fade. This could adversely impact my ability to provide legal testimony regarding a traumatic incident.

- Reactions may surface during a treatment that neither my therapist nor I can fully anticipate, which may include strong emotional or physical sensations or bring memories of additional, unresolved memories.

- Emotional material may continue to surface after a treatment session and give indication of other incidents that need to be addressed.

- My practitioner may refer me to other practitioners who have specific skills to help with problem areas beyond his/her scope of practice.

- Light touch may be involved in assessment with clinical kinesiology (also known as muscle testing) for which I can choose to give permission or not. In addition, my practitioner may use selected touch to facilitate an intervention but will always ask for my full permission before using touch.

- I will be learning personal self-care with my own energy system as part of the therapeutic process.

I have considered the above information before agreeing to receive an energy therapy treatment and have obtained whatever additional information or professional advice I consider necessary to make an informed decision. I choose to participate in energy therapy of my own free will and know I have the right to cease using these methods at any time. I agree to take full responsibility for my self-care by sharing any discomforts or questions I have with my practitioner as quickly as possible

My signature acknowledges my choice to consent to the new and innovative approaches of energy therapy my practitioner offers. My consent is free from pressure or influence from any person or group.

Client Signature_____.

Practitioner Signature_____.

Date_____.

II. Sample Client Release of Information to
Another Medical or Therapeutic Professional for Planning of Care

I_____ (name of client) herewith give my energy therapy practitioner, _____ _____ (name of practitioner), permission to release information to _____ (a designated other healthcare professional) about my condition to assist in planning for my optimal care.

I understand that the information will be limited to what is needed for my best medical or psychological care and will be kept strictly in confidence by both parties.

Client Signature_____.

Date_____.

Witness (if wished or needed)

_____.

Appendix C

Leading Energy Therapy Professional Associations

Academy of Intuition Medicine
PO Box 1921
Mill Valley, CA 94942
Telephone: 415-381-1010
E-mail: Francesca@intuitionmedicine.com
Website: www.intuitionmedicine.com

American Holistic Nurses Association (AHNA)
323 N. San Francisco St., Suite 201
Flagstaff, AZ 86001
Telephone: 800-278-2462
E-mail: office@ahna.org
Website: www.ahna.org

American Polarity Therapy Association (APTA)
122N Elm St., Suite 512
Greensboro, NC 27401
Telephone: 336-574-1121
E-mail: APTAoffice@polaritytherapy.org
Website: www.polaritytherapy.org

Association for Comprehensive Energy Psychology (ACEP)
349 W. Lancaster Ave. Suite 101
Haverford, PA 19401
Telephone: 619-861-ACEP (2237)
E-mail: info@energypsych.org
Website: www.energypsych.org

Emotional Freedom Technique (EFT)
c/o Energy Psychology Group
PO Box 442
Fulton, CA 95439
Telephone: 707-525-9292
Website:www.EFTUniverse.com

Healing Touch Program (HTP)
20822 Cactus Loop
San Antonio, TX 78258
Telephone: 210-497-5529
E-mail: info@HealingTouchProgram.com
Website: www.HealingTouchProgram.com
Research Website: www.HealingTouchResearch.com

International Association for Energy Healers (IAFEH)
PO Box 1904
Tualatin, OR, 97062
E-mail: linnie@iafeh.com
Website: www.iafeh.com

International Association of Reiki Professionals (IARP)
PO Box 6182
Nashua, NH 03063
Telephone: 603-831-8838
E-mail: info@iarp-reiki-association.com
Website: www.iarp-reiki-association.com

International Society for the Study of Subtle Energies and Energy
    Medicine (ISSSEEM)
11005 Ralston Rd., Suite 100D
Arvada, CO 80004-4551
Telephone: 303-425-4625
E-mail: Issseem2@comcast.net
Website: www.issseem.org

Nurse Healers-Professional Associates, International (NH-PAI)
PO Box 419
Craryville, NY 12521
Telephone: 518-325-1185
E-mail: nh-pai@therapeutictouch.org
Website: www.therapeutictouch.org

ENDNOTES

Chapter 1

1. O'Donohue, J. (2008) *To Bless the Space Between Us.* New York: Doubleday, 101.

2. Gerber, R. (2001) *Vibrational Medicine.* Rochester, VT: Bear & Co.

3. Thomas, L. (2010) *The Encyclopedia of Energy Medicine.* Minneapolis, MN: Fairview Press.

4. Hover-Kramer, D. (2009) *Healing Touch Guidebook: Practicing the Art and Science of Human Caring.* San Antonio, TX: Healing Touch Program Press, chapter 11.

5. Thomas, L., op. cit., and personal communications December 2010.

6. ACEP website: www.energypsych.org

7. EFT website: www.eftuniverse.com

8. Gallo, F. (1998) *Energy Psychology.* Boca Raton, FL: CRC Press.

9. Eden, D. (1998) *Energy Medicine.* New York: Tarcher/Putnam.

10. Oschman, J. (2002) *Energy Medicine: The scientific basis.* New York: Churchill Livingstone.

11. The U.S. Congress passed the Health Insurance Portability and Privacy Act (HIPPA) in 1996 to guarantee patient privacy in insurance and other professional communications.

Chapter 2

1. Barnes, P. M., et al. (2007) "Statistics on CAM use in the USA," Washington DC: National statistical report #12, 2.

2. Cohen, M. H. (2003) *Future Medicine.* Ann Arbor, MI: University of Michigan Press.

3. Cohen, M. H. (2009) as quoted in D. Hover-Kramer with M. Murphy, *Creating Right Relationships.* Port Angeles, WA: Behavioral Health Consultants, xviii.

4. Thomas, L. (2010) *The Encyclopedia of Energy Medicine.* Minneapolis, MN: Fairview Press.

5. The information given is summarized in D. Hover-Kramer with M. Murphy, *Creating Right Relationships.* Port Angeles, WA: Behavioral Health Consultants, 2009: 25–30.

6. Retrieved 12/20/2010 from www.nationalhealthfreedom.org/nhfa/protect_access.
   html

7. Watson, J. *Nursing: The art and science of human caring.* Boulder, CO: University of
   Colorado Press.

8. Smeeding, S. J. W., et al. (2010) "Outcome evaluation of the Veterans Affairs Salt
   Lake City Integrative Health Clinic for chronic pain and stress-related depression,
   anxiety, and post-traumatic stress disorder," *Journal of Complementary and Alternative
   Medicine* 16(8):832–835. http://www.liebertonline.com/doi/pdfplus/10.1089/
   acm.2009.0510

9. MacIntyre, B., et al. (2010) "Healing Touch in coronary artery bypass surgery recovery," *Energy Magazine,* September 2010.

10. Dr. Larry Stoler and Katie Oberlin, RN, described Whole Health Chicago for me in
    June 2010. Website: www.wholehealthchicago.com.

Chapter 3

1. Thomas, L. (2010) *The Encyclopedia of Energy Medicine.* Minneapolis, MN: Fairview
   Press, 6.

2. Exact legal terminology given by attorney Midge Murphy in personal communications 2005-2009.

3. Cohen, M. H. (1998) *Complementary and Alternative Medicine: Legal boundaries and
   regulatory perspectives.* Baltimore, MD: John Hopkins University Press.

4. Shouten, H., and Cohen, M. H., "Legal perspectives in integrative medicine,"
   Integrative Medicine 2(4):152–158.

Chapter 4

1. Quinn, J., "Holding sacred space: The nurse as healing environment," *Holistic Nursing
   Practice* 6:42–29. Also Quinn, J., and Strelkauskas, A. J., "Psychoimmunological
   effects of TT on practitioners of and recently bereaved recipients," *Advances in
   Nursing Science* 15:13–26.

2. Figley, C. R., ed. (2002) *Treating Compassion Fatigue.* New York: Routledge.

3. Center for Nursing Advocacy, "What is the nursing shortage and why does it exist?"
   retrieved April 2009 from www.nursingadvocacy.org/faq/nursing shortage.html

4. Counseling therapists who specialize in energy psychology can be reached at
   www.energypsych.org

5. Ross, C.A. (1996) *Dissociative Identity Disorders.* New York: John Wiley.

Chapter 5

1. Kruger, J., and Dunning, D.A., "Unskilled and unaware of it: How difficulties in
   recognizing one's own incompetence lead to inflated self-assessments," *Journal of
   Personality and Social Psychology* 77:1121–1134.

2. Snow, C., and Willard, D. (1990) *I'm Dying to Take Care of You.* Redmond, WA:
   Professional Counselor Books.

3. Dennison, P. E., and Dennison, G. E. (1990) *Brain Gym.* Glendale, CA: Edu-
   Kinesthetics.

4. Hover-Kramer, D. (2002) *Creative Energies.* New York: W. W. Norton.

5. Eden, D. (1998) *Energy Medicine.* New York: Tarcher/Putnam.

Chapter 6

1. Two favorite recent sources of chakra information are: Dale, C. (2009) *The Subtle Body: An encyclopedia of your energetic anatomy.* Boulder, CO: Sounds True; and Judith, A. (2006) *Waking the Global Heart: Humanity's rite of passage from the love of power to the power of love.* Santa Rosa, CA: Elite Books.

2. Concepts about right use of power are derived from Barstow, C. (2006) *Right Use of Power: The heart of ethics.* Boulder, CO: Many Realms Publishing.

3. Leskowitz, E., "The impact of group heart rhythm on target subject physiology," *Subtle Energies and Energy Medicine* 18(3):1–10.

4. Legal information quoted here is from personal communications with Midge Murphy and included in D. Hover-Kramer with M. Murphy, *Creating Right Relationships.* Port Angeles, WA: Behavioral Health Consultants, 2005-2009.

5. The U.S. Congress passed the Health Insurance Portability and Accountability Act (HIPAA) in 1996 to guarantee patient privacy in insurance and other professional communications.

Chapter 7

1. Krieger, D. (2004) *Therapeutic Touch as Transpersonal Healing.* New York: Lantern Books, 2.

2. *Ibid.,* 20.

Chapter 8

1. Thomas, L. (2010) *The Encyclopedia of Energy Medicine.* Minneapolis, MN: Fairview Press, 8.

2. Rocky Mt. Skeptics (www.rockymountianskeptics.com) and Quackwatch (www. Quackwatch.com) are two of the leading organizations dedicated to debunking energy modalities.

3. Aron, E. (1996) "Counseling the Highly Sensitive Person," *Journal of Human Development* 28:7.

4. Peck, S. D., "The effectiveness of TT for decreasing pain in elders with degenerative arthritis," *Journal of Holistic Nursing* 15(2):176–198.

5. Heidt, P., "The effect of TT on anxiety levels in hospitalized patients," *Nursing Research* 10(1):32–37.

Chapter 9

1. M. Murphy in D. Hover-Kramer with M. Murphy, *Creating Right Relationships.* Port Angeles, WA: Behavioral Health Consultants, 2009: 95–96.

2. *Ibid.,* 98.

Chapter 10

1. Taylor, K. (1995) *The Ethics of Caring.* Santa Cruz, CA: Hanford Mead.

2. Jung, C. G. (1971) *The Portable Jung.* New York: Penguin Press.

3. Grof, S. (1985) *Beyond the Brain.* Albany, NY: State University of New York.

4. Eliade, M. (1964) *Shamanism: Archaic traditions of ecstasy.* Princeton, NJ: Princeton University Press.

5. Wilber, K. (1996) *A Brief History of Everything.* Boston, MA: Shambhala.

6. Doidge, N. (2007) *The Brain that Changes Itself.* New York: Penguin Books.

7. Maslow, A. (1971) *The Further Reaches of Human Nature.* New York: Penguin Books.

8. For information about a large and growing number of psychotherapists who practice energy approaches, visit the practitioner listing at www.energypsych.org

9. Grof, S., and Grof, C. (1989) *Spiritual Emergency.* New York: J. P. Tarcher.

10. Pope, K. S., and Vasquez, M. J. T. (1991) *Ethics in Psychotherapy.* San Francisco, CA: Jossey-Bass, 131.

Chapter 11

1. Myss, C. (2001) *The Sacred Contract.* New York: Harmony Books.

2. *Ibid.,* 4.

3. Jung, C. G. (1971) *The Portable Jung.* New York: Penguin Press.

4. Karpman, S., "Fairytales and script drama analysis," *Transactional Analysis Bulletin* 7(27):39–43. Also discussed in James, M., and Jongeward, D. (1973) *Born to Win.* Reading, MA: Addison-Wesley.

5. Wylie, M. S., "The Ethical Therapist: Looking for fenceposts," *Family Therapy Networker* 26:2.

Chapter 12

1. Pert, C. (1997) *Molecules of Emotion.* New York: Charles Scribner's Sons.

2. Gallo, F. (2005) *Energy Psychology.* New York: W. W. Norton.

3. Feinstein, D., "The case for energy psychology," *Psychotherapy Networker* 15(6):1–6; retrieved from http://www.psychotherapynetworker.org/magazine/currentissue/1155-the-case-for-energy-psychology

4. Benson, H. (1996) *Timeless Healing.* New York: Simon & Schuster.

5. Oschman, J. (2002) *Energy Medicine: The scientific basis.* New York: Churchill Livingstone, 78.

6. Seligman, M. (2002) *Authentic Happiness.* New York: Free Press.

7. M. Murphy, personal communication with author concerning marketing materials, June 2008; also presentation at ACEP annual conference, June 2010.

8. Gruder, D. (2005) *Energy Psychology Essentials.* Del Mar, CA: Willingness Works.

Chapter 13

1. van der Kolk, B. (1996) *Traumatic Stress.* New York: Guilford.

2. Hartung, J., and Galvin, M. (2003) *Energy Psychology and EMDR.* New York: W. W. Norton.

3. Hover-Kramer, D. (2009) *Second Chance at Your Dream.* Santa Rosa, CA: Energy Psychology Press.

4. Callahan, R. (2001) *Tapping the Healer Within.* Lincolnwood, IL: Contemporary Press.

5. Heidt, P., "Effects of Therapeutic Touch on anxiety levels of hospitalized patients," Nursing Research 10(1):32–37.

6. Peck, S. D., "The effectiveness of Therapeutic Touch for decreasing pain in elders with degenerative arthritis," *Journal of Holistic Nursing* 15(2):176–198.

7. Gayne, D., and Toyne, J., "The effects of Therapeutic Touch and relaxation techniques in reducing anxiety," *Archives of Psychiatric Nursing* 8(3):184–189.

8. Hughes, P. et al., "Therapeutic Touch with psychiatric adolescent patients," *Journal of Holistic Nursing* 14(1):6–23.

9. Personal communication with attorney Midge Murphy regarding liabilities associated with making referrals, June 2009.

10. Dennison, D. (1994) *Brain Gym for Business.* Ventura, CA: Edu-Kinesthetics.

Chapter 14

1. An example of an energy modality becoming increasingly visible to the public is Hover-Kramer, D. (2011) *Healing Touch: Essential energy medicine for yourself and others.* Boulder, CO: Sounds True.

2. Feinstein, D. (2004) *Energy Psychology Interactive.* Ashland, OR: Innersource. And personal communication Energy Psychology Conference, Toronto, Ontario, November 2008.

3. Thomas, L. (2010) *The Encyclopedia of Energy Medicine.* Minneapolis, MN: Fairview Press, 6.

4. Insurance for practitioners of many of the most prominent energy modalities is available through Healing Touch Professional Association: www.htprofessionalassociation.com

5. Macy, J., and Brown, M. Y. (1998) *Coming Back to Life: Practices to reconnect our lives, our world.* Gabriola Island, BC: New Society Publishers.

6. The Dalai Lama (1999) *Ethics for a New Millennium.* New York: Riverhead Books.

7. O'Donohue, J. last lines of "For Courage," in (2008) *To Bless the Space Between Us.* New York: Doubleday, 108.

GLOSSARY

Anchoring is a psychotherapeutic term for using touch to remember a message or to give a nonverbal signal.

Archetype refers to a basic human pattern or type that is often seen and repeated throughout history; examples, Mother, Martyr, Saboteur, Healer.

Assessment is the process of collecting pertinent information about the client by using observation, a hand scan, and energetic and intuitive skills to assist in planning and implementing energetic interventions.

Attuning is the process of consciously entering into an energetic connection with the client through the use of touch or intention. Attuning is done after the practitioner centers and grounds her/himself and in implementing energy healing methods.

Aura is the metaphysical term for the human energy field, or biofield, that surrounds and penetrates the physical body. It is electromagnetic (nonmaterial) in nature. The aura is thought to be created through the spinning and vibrations of the major chakras.

Balancing is a term used to describe realignment of the biofield and energy centers toward their natural, highest vibrational frequencies and functions.

Biofield is the scientific term for the vibrational emanations that surround and interpenetrate the human body, also known as the human energy field or aura. The biofield can be measured by SQID (superconducting quantum interference device) and demonstrated through Kirlian photography and other scientific instrumentation.

Caring forms the theoretical basis of most energetic practices and is described most fully by leading nursing and interdisciplinary theorist Dr. Jean Watson.

Centering is the practitioner's art of being fully present to the client while at the same time being connected and focused within and open to intuitive guidance. Ongoing practices of meditation enhance and deepen centering. Focus on the breath assists the centering process.

Chakra is the Sanskrit term for the energy vortices, or energy centers, of the human body. Chakras appear to control the intake and outflow of energy to specific regions of the body. The seven major chakras form an energy matrix that supports physical, emotional, mental, and spiritual health and reflects developmental aspects of consciousness.

Consultant refers to a professional who is sought out for his or her expertise in addressing practice issues or dilemmas. Different from a friend or mentor, a consultant is able to be objective and identify many aspects of a situation in order to assist professionals to become effective. Unlike a supervisor, a consultant does not carry legal responsibility for the professional's actions as a result of consultation.

Countertransference happens when the caregiver begins to respond to a client in nonobjective ways, as, for example, in seeing a client as a helpless child or as a bossy parent.

Energy blockage is a general term that refers to the interruption or constriction of the natural flow patterns within the human energy system. It also can be used to describe a compromised or diminished chakra, asymmetry in the biofield, or nonpolarity of the meridian flows. Chronic blockage is believed to lead to illness and *dis-ease* in the body-mind-spirit.

Energy center is interchangeable with the term "chakra" and describes a specific center of consciousness that permits flow of energy into and out from the entire biofield.

Energy healing is the broad term used to describe interventions utilizing aspects of the human energy system (biofield, chakras, meridians, flows, grids) to bring about increased human functioning. The methods include releasing energetic blockages and repatterning, connecting, opening, balancing, or aligning the energies of the person. There are over 250 known modalities of energy healing currently in use.

Energy medicine is the broad term that encompasses a wide variety of treatments to assist persons in relieving their physical, emotional, or mental suffering through the use of one or more aspects of the human energy system.

Energy psychology is a specific branch of energy medicine that predominantly addresses emotional and psychological issues by utilizing one or several of the components of the human energy system.

Healing is the ongoing evolving dynamic of moving toward ever greater levels of integration of body, mind, and spirit. Healing may bring about one or more outcomes, such as physical wellness, emotional integration, mental clarity, or spiritual connectedness.

Higher Power is the name that many practitioners use to refer to the Source of Life, Creator of All That Is, Universal Energy Field, Spirit, the One, Unifying Force, Ground of Being, and God (for Good Orderly Direction).

Higher sense perception is knowledge coming from beyond the physical senses of seeing, hearing, tasting, smelling, and touching. Examples are intuition, clairvoyance, and clairaudience. This sense of knowing comes from within and is often spontaneous and unpredicted. The prevalence of these perceptions has been growing in public awareness over the last century.

Human energy system (HES) encompasses the entire interactive dynamic of human subtle energies consisting of the chakras, the multidimensional biofield, the meridians, and related acupoints, grids, and other flow pathways. The human vibrational matrix of subtle electromagnetic energy flows is assumed to consist of additional aspects that have not yet been identified through scientific means.

Intention is the holding of positive goodwill on behalf of the client for his or her highest good. Clear intention allows practitioners to focus on their inner awareness and to accomplish specific interventions without attachment to a specific outcome.

Life essence is a general term used to describe the vital life force of a person and the form of consciousness that is believed to continue beyond physical life. Related terms include life energy, *qi* (pronounced "chee"), *ki, prana,* universal energy, or *spiritus.*

Meditation is the practice of raising the vibrations of ordinary consciousness through a disciplined practice of stilling the body, emotions, and mind to become calm, centered, receptive, and focused. Advanced meditative practices lead to experiences of guidance beyond usual linear perceptions and accelerate intuitive perceptions.

Mentor is a friend or colleague who has more experience and is willing to help a new practitioner to know details of establishing an energy therapy practice.

Method is a synonym for technique, intervention, or treatment used in the practice of energy therapies.

Practice describes the actual parameters of a professional's work based on an identified knowledge base and experience.

Psychoenergetic healing describes a form of healing practice that interrelates psychological insights with energetic treatment and defines the work of energy psychotherapists.

Somatic means "of, relating to, or affecting the body" and is an adjective used to designate body-oriented therapies.

Spiritual practice is differentiated from specific religious beliefs and describes each person's unique means of accessing perceptions that go beyond the ego self. Spiritual practices include centering, meditating, praying, breathing purposefully, grounding, setting one's intention, journaling, artistic expression, learning to trust intuition, and many others.

Therapy refers to specific practices and interventions that bring about relief from human distress; therapies can be somatic (body-related), psychologically oriented as in psychotherapy, or medically related as in chemotherapy. "Physical therapy" is a specific discipline that is licensed.

Transference describes the establishment of rapport with a practitioner and, when positive, is frequently an effective connection that helps clients make changes. Negative transference can limit or inhibit therapeutic relationships, for example, when the client sees the practitioner as a bad stepparent.

Transpersonal consciousness reaches the psychospiritual realm, beyond the purely personal, and extends to the wider, spiritual dimensions of human experience. It elevates personal spiritual experiences to awareness of one's divinity and eternal being.

INDEX

A

Academy of Intuition Medicine, 222, 233
allopathic medicine, 37, 45, 141
archetypes, xiv, 130, 148, 165–172, 176, 219
Association for Comprehensive Energy Psychology (ACEP), xi, 28, 222, 234, 237

B

Benson, Herbert, 190, 240
boundaries, in practice, 29, 76, 90, 97, 114, 117, 121, 125, 127, 129, 145, 146, 160, 168, 169, 171, 172, 180, 206, 218, 238
Brain Gym, 83, 208, 238, 241

C

chakras, 26, 64, 83, 106, 114, 150, 158, 175, 189, 200, 243
  overview of functions, 87–92
  vulnerabilities, 92–97
  resolution strategies, 97–101
codependency, 79, 91, 114, 168
Cohen, Michael H., 39, 41, 227, 237, 238
complementary alternative medicine (CAM), xiii, 28, 29, 37, 39–42, 46, 48, 237
consultation, 31, 49, 51, 57, 61, 78, 92, 94, 96, 100, 101, 105, 112, 113, 114, 117, 121, 125, 132, 146, 159, 160, 195, 196, 202, 204, 206, 212, 213, 215, 218, 223, 244

contract, 31, 127, 132, 134–5, 142, 145, 163–166, 172, 173, 175, 193, 206, 227, 240
countertransference, 77–78, 171, 244

D

Dalai Lama, 225, 227, 241
Dale, Cyndi, xvii–xxi, 183, 227, 239

E

Eden, Donna, 83, 227, 237
Eliade, Mircea, 154, 240
Emotional Freedom Technique (EFT), 28, 234, 237
energy medicine, xvii, 26–38, 43, 44, 46, 187, 199, 200, 201, 221, 223, 227, 234, 240, 245
energy psychology, xi, xvi, 28, 45, 83, 138, 188, 193, 220, 222, 233, 237, 238, 240, 245
ethics, xiii, xvi, xvii, 30, 31, 32, 39, 47, 48, 54, 92, 125, 168, 188, 195, 210, 221, 222, 223, 227, 239, 240, 241,
Eye Movement Desensitization and Reprocessing (EMDR), 200, 241

F

Federal Trade Commission (FTC), 40, 50
Feinstein, David, 220, 227, 240, 241
Food and Drug Administration (FDA), 40, 50
Freud, Sigmund, 192

G
Gallo, Fred, 28, 237, 240
Grof, Stanislav, 154, 240

H
Healing Touch, xi, xix, 27, 42, 45, 69,
    138, 188, 200, 202, 222, 223,
    227, 238, 241
Healing Touch Program, xi, xvi, 38,
    234, 237, 241
HIPPA (Health Insurance Portability
    and Privacy Act), 33, 237

I
integrative healthcare (IHC), xviii, 36,
    112
    development of, 37–43
    models of, 44–45, 112
International Association for Energy
    Healers (IAFEH), 28
intuition, xviii, 29, 73, 84, 88, 91, 96,
    100, 103–105, 108, 110, 130,
    152, 164, 176, 179, 218, 219,
    245, 246,

J
Jung, Carl Gustav, 75, 79, 154, 155,
    165, 166, 192, 240,

K
Krieger, Dolores, 109, 239

L
legal considerations, xx, 32, 47–54
    concerning chakra vulnerabilities,
        92–97
    regarding referrals, 204–205

M
Macy, Joanna, 224, 241
marketing, xx, 49, 98, 126, 192–193,
    206, 211, 218, 219, 240
Maslow, Abraham, 192, 240
morals, 30
mind-body interactions, 26, 129, 191,
    194, 201
multidimensional healing, 28, 109, 127,
    171, 204, 245
Murphy, Midge, xiii, 140, 237, 238,
    239, 240, 241

Myss, Caroline, 163, 164, 166, 170,
    171, 227, 240

N
National Center for Complementary
    and Alternative Medicine
    (NCCAM), 37, 38, 46
National Health Freedom Coalition
    (NHFC), 40, 41
National Institutes of Health (NIH),
    37, 38
Nightingale, Florence, 192
nonordinary states of consciousness,
    xiv, 29, 97, 108, 109, 126, 148,
    149–162, 171, 177, 204

O
O'Donohue, John, 25, 225, 228,
    237, 241
Ornish, Dean, 44
Oschman, James, 190, 228, 237, 240
overconfidence, 76, 112
overinvolvement, 61, 78

P
posttraumatic stress disorder (PTSD),
    44, 114, 193,
power differential, 55, 90, 94, 104, 114,
    124, 127, 130–131, 143, 167,
    206, 207, 209,
principles, 30–32, 39, 42, 46, 48, 92,
    111, 124, 134, 197, 199, 207,
    217, 218, 222
professionalism, xiv, xxi, 30, 31, 32,
    92, 223
professional organizations, importance
    of, 45–46, 192, 221, 233–235

Q
qi, 76, 83, 107, 109, 115, 141, 161,
    171, 190, 246

R
referrals,
    need for, xx, 43, 57, 125, 195, 196,
        203–204
    legal considerations in, 204–205, 241
repatterning, 27, 245

S

scope of practice, 51, 93, 96, 97, 112,
        124, 126, 139, 142, 146, 147,
        160, 194, 203, 204, 221, 229
seasonal affective disorder (SAD), 83
self-care, xiii, xx, 30, 37, 63–73,
        81, 113, 115, 128, 136, 143,
        146, 150, 161, 168, 171, 189,
        196, 200
Seligman, Martin, 192, 240
Shealy, Norman, 164
standards, 31. Also called standards of
        care, standards of practice, ethical/
        professional
Stoler, Larry, 45, 238

T

Taylor, Kylea, 150,227, 240
Therapeutic Touch, 27, 42, 69, 109,
        138, 241
Thomas, Linnie, xvi, 27, 28, 39, 47,
        228, 237, 238, 239, 241
trance, 150, 152, 155, 160, 177,
        178,190, 200, 222, 239,
transference, 76–77, 90, 113, 114, 124,
        149, 160, 167, 171, 247
trauma, 27, 28, 43, 68, 69, 111, 114,
        128, 130, 134, 140,145, 151,
        155, 156, 156, 157, 178, 180,
        189, 200, 203, 230,

V

values, xiii, xviii, xx, 25, 26, 30, 31, 32,
        39, 46, 48, 75, 76, 89, 91, 94,
        100, 123, 164, 167, 169, 188,
        217, 222, 225,

W

Watson, Jean, 42, 228, 238, 244
Wilber, Ken, 154, 240